NATIONAL GEOGRAPHIC KiDS

EXTREME RECORDS

THE TALLEST, WEIRDEST, *FASTEST*, COOLEST STUFF ON PLANET EARTH!

JULIE BEER AND MICHELLE HARRIS

NATIONAL GEOGRAPHIC
WASHINGTON, D.C.

GET READY TO GO TO THE EXTREME

It's time to set the records straight!

In *National Geographic Extreme Records*, you'll explore the most out-there records the world has to offer—from the tallest mountain to the deepest cave, from the smallest drone to the fastest trains, from the most dangerous thing underfoot to the most dangerous jobs around, and from the oddest ancient creatures to the teeniest, deadliest, and most extreme animals on Earth. In every chapter, check out more of our planet's epic records in "Case Study," "Spotlight," and "Creature Feature"; watch two extremes go head-to-head in "Smackdown Central"; and check out long-ago extremes in "Blast From the Past." And at the end of each chapter, it's all about the fun and games: Rank the extremes you read about, do some myth-busting, and even try out an extremely delicious ice-cream recipe!

Are you ready for some action-packed fun? Then turn the page and dive in!

NATIONAL GEOGRAPHIC
PHOTOGRAPHER
CARSTEN PETER

CHAPTER 1

WE'RE SIZING UP SOME OF THE
BIGGEST, HEAVIEST, TALLEST, AND *MOST MASSIVE*
THINGS IN THE WORLD.

Get ready to meet the mind-blowing marvels that run extra large—from huge animals to colossal coasters to supersize aircraft to a pool that seems to stretch as far as the eye can see. Here are the giants of Earth and beyond.

BIGGEST

MAUNA LOA

Think the tallest mountain on Earth is Everest? Surprise! It's Mauna Loa, an active volcano in Hawaii, U.S.A. Now before you demand a re-measure, here's the scoop: At 56,000 feet (17,170 m) from its peak to its base, which is depressed 26,200 feet (7,990 m) below the ocean floor, Mauna Loa is almost twice as tall as Mt. Everest's 29,035 feet (8,850 m). So why doesn't it look like it? Because only a quarter of Mauna Loa is above water! Although Everest's summit is the highest above sea level, Mauna Loa takes the prize from top to bottom. To further bruise Everest's ego, Mauna Loa's neighbor, Mauna Kea, also towers: From the ocean floor to its summit, Mauna Kea stands 32,000 feet (9,750 m).

MAUNA LOA IS **SO MASSIVE** THAT IT ACTUALLY **SUNK THE OCEAN FLOOR** 26,000 FEET (8,000 M) IN THE SHAPE OF AN **INVERTED CONE.**

VOLCANO TYPE:
SHIELD VOLCANO

HEIGHT BASE TO SUMMIT:
56,000 FEET (17,170 M)

HEIGHT ABOVE SEA LEVEL:
13,680 FEET (4,170 M)

ABOVE-WATER SURFACE AREA:
HALF OF THE ISLAND OF HAWAII

ERUPTIONS SINCE 1843: **33**

LAST ERUPTION: **1984**

NAME'S MEANING:
"LONG MOUNTAIN"

BIGGER THAN BIG

Check out some record holders that "outsized" their competitors.

BIGGEST **CITY**
TOKYO

Imagine a city that covers only a quarter of the New York City metropolitan area but is home to more people than all of Canada: That's Tokyo—the world's most populated city. Some 37 million people live in Tokyo and its surrounding metro area. To get around Japan's capital city, many people travel by train; the cars are so crowded that there are official train "pushers" whose job it is to make sure everyone gets onboard so the doors can shut.

TALLEST **FERRIS WHEEL**
HIGH ROLLER

Talk about reinventing the wheel! Covered in more than 2,000 lights, the 550-foot (168-m) High Roller observation wheel, located in Las Vegas, Nevada, U.S.A., isn't your average county fair Ferris wheel. Passengers sit in one of the wheel's 28 "pods"—glass cabins that provide a 360-degree view. Adrenaline-seekers be warned: This is a leisurely ride. It takes 30 minutes for the wheel to complete one revolution—that's just one foot (0.3 m) per second!

BIGGEST **PLANE**
AIRBUS A380

This is one *jumbo* jet. The Airbus A380, the world's largest commercial aircraft, has a double-decker cabin and enough space to hold 853 passengers! At 262 feet (80 m), its wingspan is as wide as 30 parking spaces. The A380 can cruise for more than 9,000 miles (14,484 km) without refueling, so it's no surprise it takes a lot to fill the tank: It can hold 81,890 gallons (310,000 L) of fuel—that's about 5,460 refills on a family car!

LARGEST **SWIMMING POOL**
SAN ALFONSO DEL MAR

Want to hit the pool and swim a few laps? Put on your goggles and clear your afternoon! Just one lap in the San Alfonso del Mar seawater pool, located in Algarrobo, Chile, is the equivalent of 20 laps in an Olympic-size pool. It holds 66 million gallons (250 million L) of water and is so big small sailboats can cruise on it!

From the tallest grazer to the heaviest gourd, you can't beat these biggies.

LONGEST **BRIDGE**

DANYANG-KUNSHAN GRAND BRIDGE

Don't try to hold your breath when you cross *this* bridge! It's more than 100 miles (160 km) long! The Danyang-Kunshan Grand Bridge, the world's longest, connects the Chinese cities of Shanghai and Nanjing. The bridge is mostly used as a high-speed railway, carrying trains that travel as fast as 187 miles an hour (300 km/h).

HEAVIEST **PUMPKIN**

CUCURBITA MAXIMA

Think of the guts you'd have to scoop out to turn this supersize squash into a jack-o'-lantern! The *Cucurbita maxima* is considered the largest variety of pumpkin, with individuals weighing in at more than 2,600 pounds (1,179 kg). That's the size of a small car! Giant pumpkins can grow almost 50 pounds (23 kg) a day during their peak growing season, and their seeds aren't always cheap: Some people will pay up to $1,000 for one seed from a champion pumpkin.

TALLEST LAND ANIMAL

GIRAFFE

In a back-to-back contest, this marvelous mammal wins the title of Earth's tallest land creature. Stretching up to 19 feet (5.8 m) skyward, a giraffe sports legs that are longer than many humans are tall—about six feet (1.8 m)! Its lengthy neck helps it reach leaves that other animals can't, but so does its tongue: At 21 inches (53 cm) long, it helps pull even the most hard-to-reach leaves off a branch.

TALLEST TREE

COAST REDWOOD

One surefire way to get a kink in your neck: trying to tilt your head back far enough to spot the tip of a coast redwood tree! It's impossible to glimpse the top of these incredible evergreens—which stand as high as 379 feet (116 m)—from the forest floor. Coast redwoods grow along the Pacific Coast between central California and southern Oregon. They live up to 2,000 years and grow in groups— forming a natural wind protection to prevent toppling.

RACE TO THE TOP: THE **WORLD'S** TALLEST BUILDINGS

N ew York's Empire State Building held the title of "world's tallest building" from the time it was completed in 1931 through 1970, when the World Trade Center's north tower beat it out. Since the 1970s, the race to be the tallest has been a series of one-uppings. For several years, Burj Khalifa, located in Dubai, United Arab Emirates, has kept a firm grasp on the title. The skyscraper stands more than 2,716.5 feet (828 m) and contains a whopping 163 stories. (It also boasts the highest elevator!) But Burj Khalifa doesn't stand alone—these high-rises also reach new heights.

SUPERSIZE STATS ABOUT BURJ KHALIFA

• The weight of the concrete used to build Burj Khalifa is equivalent to **100,000 elephants.**
• The total weight of aluminum used during construction is equivalent to that of **five Airbus A380 aircraft.**
• If you chose to take the stairs instead of the elevator, you would climb **2,909 steps** to get to level 160.
• There are **3,000 parking spaces** in the building's basement levels.

TOWERING HEIGHTS: Three Towers That Aim High

SHANGHAI TOWER, CHINA

HEIGHT: 2,073 FEET (632 M)

CLAIM TO FAME: Located in Shanghai's financial district, the second tallest building in the world was built to withstand the wind effect that sways skyscrapers: Its tapered spiral design allows wind to swirl around the structure.

TAIPEI 101, TAIPEI, TAIWAN

HEIGHT: 1,670 FEET (509 M)

CLAIM TO FAME: The tallest building in the world from 2004 to 2007, Taipei 101 was dethroned by Burj Khalifa, but it will never lose its unique look. Its design was inspired by traditional Chinese architecture and resembles a pagoda.

ONE WORLD TRADE CENTER, NEW YORK CITY

HEIGHT (INCLUDING ANTENNA): 1,776 FEET (541 M)

CLAIM TO FAME: Does the number 1,776 look familiar? It should! 1776 is the year the Declaration of Independence was signed—fitting for a building originally called the Freedom Tower. The tallest building in the Western Hemisphere, One World Trade Center is 104 stories.

COLOSSAL COASTERS

A strong stomach is a must if you plan on climbing aboard one of these roller coasters. Here are four record-setting amusement park rides thrill-seekers will want to stand in line for!

TALLEST

KINGDA KA, JACKSON, NEW JERSEY, U.S.A.

The king of all coasters, Kingda Ka reaches 456 feet (139 m) in the sky; to get there, the climb is 90 degrees straight up! Put your hands in the air for this 50-second ride, which reaches speeds of 128 miles an hour (206 km/h).

LONGEST

STEEL DRAGON 2000, MIE PREFECTURE, JAPAN

Never want a ride to end? Then Steel Dragon 2000 is just the ticket. It spans 1.5 miles (2.4 km) of track and lasts about three minutes—that's eons in roller coaster time! But don't worry, there's still plenty of adrenaline: It has a 310-foot (94-m) drop and reaches speeds of 95 miles an hour (153 km/h).

FASTEST

FORMULA ROSSA, ABU DHABI, UNITED ARAB EMIRATES

Start your engines! Formula Rossa, the world's fastest roller coaster, was designed to look like a Ferrari Formula One car. And it handles like one, too: The ride goes from zero to 149 miles an hour (240 km/h) in 4.9 seconds. The wind on this 92-second ride is so intense that safety glasses are required!

HIGHEST LOOP

FULL THROTTLE, VALENCIA, CALIFORNIA, U.S.A.

Gravity check! The world's fastest and tallest looping roller coaster, Full Throttle tops out at 160 feet (49 m). After you make your way back down the loop, you're bolted right back up—at 70 miles an hour (113 km/h)— but in reverse. What goes up must come down!

OUT-OF-THIS-WORLD
MOONS

Think Earth is a big place? Wait until you see how some out-of-this-world bodies measure up! Check out where Earth's moon and other giant orbiting satellites fall on the grand scale.

GANYMEDE

Who couldn't swoon over all of Jupiter's moons? The fifth planet from the sun has 53 in all (more than any other planet in our solar system), including the largest moon in the solar system, Ganymede. This supersize satellite is three-quarters the diameter of Mars and is covered in an ice shell about 497 miles (800 km) thick.

TITAN

Titan, Saturn's largest moon, is the second largest moon in the solar system—larger even than the planet Mercury. It's the only moon in the solar system to have a thick atmosphere, and it has a liquid ocean beneath its surface, possibly composed of water and ammonia.

CALLISTO

Jupiter's second largest moon (and the third largest in the solar system), Callisto shines bright—twice as bright as Earth's moon. And it has stood the test of time: It is the most heavily cratered object in the solar system. Visiting Callisto would be a bit chilly—the moon's mean surface temperature is -218°F (-139°C).

IO

Slightly larger than Earth's moon, Io is Jupiter's third largest moon (and the fourth largest in the solar system). It is also the most volcanically active place in the solar system: Volcanic plumes 190 miles (300 km) high rise from the surface, which is also covered in lava lakes.

EARTH'S MOON

To us Earthlings, the moon ranks number one—after all, it is the brightest object in the night sky. But in a lineup of moons in our solar system, it ranks fifth— at least in terms of size. One-quarter the diameter of Earth, it's the only place out- side our planet that humans (12 in all) have stood upon.

POLAR BEARS:
BIG
BEAR
OF THE
NORTH

Tipping the scale at 1,600 pounds (725 kg), polar bears are the heaviest of all bears. But don't peg them as big couch potatoes. Roaming across Arctic ice sheets, polar bears have been seen hundreds of miles from land, swimming and floating on ice. They have a thick layer of fat and a water-repellent coat to help keep them warm—fur even grows on the bottom of their paws to protect their pads from ice! Another built-in warming device: Their skin is black, which absorbs sunlight. Polar bears spend about half of their time hunting their favorite food—seals—because less than 2 percent of their hunts are successful.

NEWBORN POLAR BEARS ARE THE SIZE AND WEIGHT OF A LOAF OF BREAD.

BATTLE OF THE BIGGEST

There's big ... and then there's ginormous. In a throw-down of epic proportions, there can be only one winner.

These hard-to-miss iconic landmarks certainly grab tourists' attention, but only one can win this competition—and the award goes to Big Ben! The clock tower that houses the massive hour bell measures in at 320 feet (97.5 m). If only the Statue of Liberty could stand on her tiptoes! From the ground to the tip of her torch, Lady Liberty just misses the mark, at 305 feet (93 m).

WINNER

STATUE OF LIBERTY **VS.** BIG BEN

The name is a bit of a give-away—giant pandas weigh in at as much as 250 pounds (113 kg). Red pandas (who aren't pandas at all; they belong to the Ailuridae family, a family they are the only living member of) tip the scales at a mere 14 pounds (6 kg)! So giant pandas win this one paws down, with one catch: When they're born, giant and red pandas are about the same size!

WINNER

RED PANDA **VS.** GIANT PANDA

HARRY POTTER vs. LORD OF THE RINGS

WINNER

Expelliarmus, *Lord of the Rings!* The eight *Harry Potter* movies combined made more at the box office ($7.7 billion worldwide) than the *Lord of the Rings* and *The Hobbit* trilogies combined ($5.84 billion worldwide). And the *Harry Potter* world is just getting started: *Fantastic Beasts and Where to Find Them* has already worked its magic in theaters, and there are several more in that series on the way. Accio, movie tickets!

TORTOISE vs. HARE

TIE

We're not talking speed here, we're talking size, and in that category we have a tie! Believe it or not, there are some bunnies that run extra long. From ear to toe the Flemish giant rabbit can grow as tall as four feet (1.2 m)! And the Galápagos tortoise, the world's largest species of tortoise, averages about the same length. Finally, an even competition between these two!

GREAT BARRIER REEF

"Great" is putting it mildly when it comes to the Great Barrier Reef, the world's largest coral reef system. And these numbers prove it!

STRETCHES **1,249 MILES** (2,010 KM)

COVERS **132,974 SQUARE MILES** (344,400 SQ KM), ABOUT THE SAME SIZE AS **JAPAN**

26

INCLUDES

- **3,000** CORAL REEFS
- **600** CONTINENTAL ISLANDS

HOME TO

- **1,625** TYPES OF **FISH**
- **133** VARIETIES OF **SHARKS** AND **RAYS**
- **30** SPECIES OF WHALES, PORPOISES, AND **DOLPHINS**
- **17** SPECIES OF **SEA SNAKES**
- **600** TYPES OF SOFT AND HARD **CORAL**
- **215** SPECIES OF BIRDS THAT **VISIT** OR **NEST** THERE

A Mega Shark With a MONSTROUS BITE

CARCHAROCLES MEGALODON

LIVED DURING: **CENOZOIC ERA (20 TO 2.5 MILLION YEARS AGO)**

LENGTH: **45 TO 60 FEET (14 TO 18 M)**

WEIGHT: **UP TO 100 TONS (91 T)**

TOOTH HEIGHT: **5.7 INCHES (14 CM)**

Picture a perilous predator that's longer than a school bus, weighs more than 14 African elephants, and sports jaws large enough to swallow a small car. The description alone is enough to send shivers down your spine! Meet megalodon, an extinct shark abundant in Earth's oceans during the Cenozoic era. No one knows why megalodon—the largest predatory shark that ever lived—went extinct after its nearly 20-million-year run roaming the seas, but it may have been competition from slightly smaller and more aggressive sharks and whales. One way researchers can estimate megalodon's size is by analyzing its teeth, which were about 5.7 inches (14 cm) tall and likely used to eat whales and dolphins.

NATURE'S BIGGEST AT A GLANCE

1 LARGEST LIVING ORGANISM

Talk about a humongous fungus! One mushroom growing in Oregon's Blue Mountains covers nearly four square miles (10 sq km)—that's the equivalent of 1,665 football fields! It grows mostly underground but has fruiting bodies in the aboveground soil that are a yellow-brown color, giving it the nickname "honey fungus." It may look and sound nonthreatening, but the fungus can take over and kill plants and trees!

2 BIGGEST CANYON

The Grand Canyon, in Arizona, U.S.A., has nothing on Tibet's Yarlung Tsangpo Grand Canyon, the world's deepest canyon. Carved into granite bedrock, it's 17,000 feet (5,182 m) from top to bottom—that's three times deeper than the Arizona icon. Stretching more than 300 miles (483 km), it's also one of the longest canyons in the world.

3 TALLEST WATERFALL

The world's tallest waterfall is taller than the world's tallest building and the world's tallest roller coaster combined! Venezuela's Angel Falls drops an incredible 3,212 feet (979 m). Jungle surrounds the falls, so most people take in its sheer hugeness from a plane or helicopter.

IT'S DARK
DOWN
THERE!

Animals that live inside Mammoth Cave have adapted to the dark conditions: Eyeless cave shrimp don't grow eye structures because they don't need eyes to see. Their skin lacks pigment and appears almost translucent.

4 LARGEST RIVER

The Nile may be the world's longest river, stretching 4,132 miles (6,650 km), but the Amazon, which runs a hair shorter at 4,000 miles (6,437 km), is the largest in terms of the amount of freshwater that rolls down it. One-fifth of the world's freshwater flow is contained in the Amazon Basin. All that water dilutes the ocean's saltiness more than 100 miles (160 km) from shore.

5 BIGGEST CAVE SYSTEM

Mammoth Cave in Kentucky, U.S.A., has earned the title of longest cave system in the world ... and scientists haven't even finished measuring how long it is! Some 400 miles (644 km) of twisting labyrinth of limestone caves have been explored. It's estimated the first human entered Mammoth Cave 4,000 years ago.

6 LARGEST OCEAN

The Pacific Ocean wins this one hands down. All of Earth's continents—30 percent of Earth's surface!—could fit in the Pacific. The Pacific covers more than 60 million square miles (155 million sq km) and is also the deepest and oldest of all the existing ocean basins. The Pacific Basin is known as the "Ring of Fire" because of the volcanic activity that occurs where the tectonic plates meet.

WORLD'S BIGGEST (RADIO) TELESCOPE

FAST IS THE SIZE OF 30 FOOTBALL FIELDS.

China's Five Hundred Meter Aperture Spherical Telescope (FAST) is the world's largest radio telescope. (Its namesake 500-meter [1,650-foot] diameter is almost 40 percent larger than the second largest telescope of its kind, located in Puerto Rico.) The job of the $180 million dish—which scans deep outer space gathering radio signals—is to find low-frequency gravitational waves, dark matter, and fast radio bursts ... and to listen for signals that may have been made by faraway alien civilizations. Located in China's remote, mountainous Guizhou province, FAST, which was completed in 2016, is situated miles from any towns because "radio silence" is needed to pick up accurate signals.

HERE'S THE
BIG FINISH

Can you put these oversize chapter
champs in order from tallest to shortest?

A

B

C

ITSY, BITSY, TEENY, AND TERRIFIC! SOME OF THE GREATEST THINGS COME IN SMALL PACKAGES.

Break out the magnifying glass and be careful where you step, because this chapter is chock-full of totally tiny treasures. From petite primates to a pint-size park, teensy tree houses, and even the coziest country—we're off on a mini adventure!

MADAME BERTHE'S MOUSE LEMUR

With perky ears, a long tail, and a body the size of a house mouse, you'd never guess that Madame Berthe's mouse lemur belongs to the same group of animals that includes humans and great apes! Believed to be the world's smallest primate, this lemur is found only in the forests of Madagascar, an island nation off the eastern coast of Africa. It isn't easy to spot the little lemur climbing on limbs in the canopy, but you can count on it spotting you. Check out those outrageous eyes—buggy peepers perfect for finding bugs at night.

TAIL LENGTH:
ABOUT 5 INCHES (12.7 CM)

BODY SIZE:
3.5 INCHES (9 CM), MINUS THE TAIL

SCIENTIFIC NAME:
MICROCEBUS BERTHAE

MADAME BERTHE'S MOUSE LEMURS CAN LOWER THEIR BODY TEMPERATURE IN THE WINTER TO SAVE ENERGY AND WATER.

HABITAT: DRY FORESTS OF MADAGASCAR

WEIGHT: 1 OUNCE (30 G)

DIET: HONEYDEW (A SUBSTANCE PRODUCED BY INSECT LARVAE), FLOWERS, FRUITS, INSECTS, CHAMELEONS, AND GECKOS

SMALL WONDERS

These record holders prove that it really is a small world after all.

SMALLEST COUNTRY
HOLY SEE (VATICAN CITY)

You could easily fit the smallest country in the world on Washington, D.C.'s National Mall. The Holy See, also known as Vatican City, is a city-state surrounded by Rome, Italy, with an area of just .17 square mile (.44 sq km). Only about 1,000 people live there, including the pope (the head of the Catholic Church), making it the third least populated country in the world. (The Cocos [Keeling] Islands and Pitcairn Islands are the only two countries with fewer people.) But the small country is a big draw for devoted Catholics, who consider it a sacred place of pilgrimage.

SMALLEST **SHARK**
DWARF LANTERN SHARK

Talk about a little fish in a big pond: The dwarf lantern shark is so small you could easily hold it in one hand. But that doesn't mean it's hard to spot—in fact, it glows! Measuring about six inches (16 cm) in length, the dwarf lantern shark has light-emitting organs along its belly and fins that help it camouflage with sunlight when feeding in shallow water—and evade any predators below. The glow also helps it attract a midnight snack: Smaller fish are lured by the glow in the dark water.

SMALLEST **LANGUAGE**
TOKI PONA

Are you good at making small talk? Well, it doesn't get much smaller than Toki Pona, the world's smallest language. Created in 2001 with a total vocabulary of 120 words that use 14 sounds, Toki Pona is said to take as little as 30 hours to master. The creator of Toki Pona, Sonya Lang, a linguist from Toronto, Canada, wanted to create a unique language that would use simple concepts with maximum meaning. Toki Pona has been learned by people around the globe, who communicate online in their new common language.

SMALLEST **SNAKE**
BARBADOS THREADSNAKE

What's long and skinny and wiggles in the dirt? Nope—not a worm, even though it might look like one. It's actually the Barbados threadsnake—thought to be the world's smallest snake. This slight serpent measures less than two toothpicks long and can be found—you guessed it!—on the Caribbean island of Barbados. First discovered in 2008, female Barbados threadsnakes produce a single elongated egg, and the hatchlings emerge already half the size of their mother.

Don't sweat the small stuff ... be amazed by it!

SMALLEST THING IN THE UNIVERSE

POINT PARTICLES

The building blocks of matter, fundamental "point particles" like quarks and electrons are so small that they can't even be broken apart. But does that actually make them the smallest things in the universe? For now, physicists haven't discovered anything smaller, but they continue to investigate whether there might be something even more micro out there.

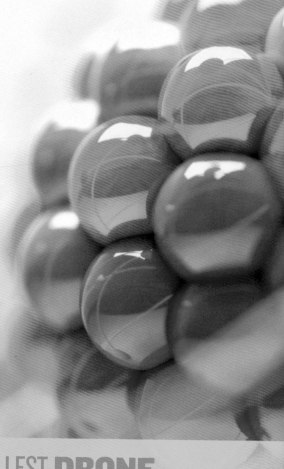

SMALLEST DRONE

PICCOLISSIMO

The smallest self-powered drone is so small it could fit on a quarter! Appropriately named Piccolissimo, the Italian word for tiniest, the drone is powered by a super small, super lightweight battery and has a mini motor that spins its body while a propeller spins in the opposite direction. It is strong enough to carry a small sensor, which researchers say could one day aid in search and rescue efforts.

SMALLEST **BONE IN HUMAN BODY**

STAPES BONE

It may be small, but it is mighty: the bittiest bone in your body is found in your middle ear. The stapes (along with the malleus and incus) work together to transmit vibrations caused by sound waves to the liquid of the inner ear. The stapes looks like a stirrup and is a mere 1/26 of an inch (1 mm).

SMALLEST **GUITAR**

THE NANOGUITAR

At roughly the size of a human blood cell, you'd have a really hard time rocking out on *this* guitar. Made in a laboratory in New York, U.S.A., the infinitesimal instrument comes complete with six strings—each of which is 50 nanometers wide. (One nanometer is one-billionth of a meter, so think *really* teeny tiny.) The guitar was made to show off the new technology available to make ultra microscopic things, which will eventually be used to make super small parts for electronics.

TINY HOUSES ARE
ENORMOUSLY
POPULAR

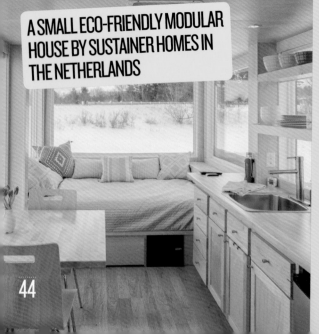

A SMALL ECO-FRIENDLY MODULAR HOUSE BY SUSTAINER HOMES IN THE NETHERLANDS

Some people are downsizing to live in homes as small as a tree house—in fact, some *are* tree houses! "Tiny houses" are generally defined as homes that are smaller than 400 square feet (37 sq m). (For comparison, the median size of a new house in the United States is 2,467 square feet [229 sq m].) But to go that small, you have to get creative. Get ready to go door-to-door to check out these adorable abodes!

COMPACT LIVING

SIZE: 188 square feet (17.5 sq m)
LOCATION: London, England
CRAZY-SMALL FEATURE:
Hidden storage under the living room/dining room floor

Imagine if you had to climb over the kitchen to get to your bed. This one-room tiny house that recently sold in London is so compact that the stairs to the loft bed are accessed by the kitchen countertop. The tiny house also features a toilet-shower room—that's right, the toilet is inside the shower stall!

ISLAND TREE HOUSE

SIZE: 101 square feet (9.4 sq m), plus a loft
LOCATION: British Columbia, Canada
CRAZY-SMALL FEATURE: A ladder to the loft that doubles as storage

Who wouldn't want to live in a tree house? That's what the owner of this tiny house, which stands 17 feet (5.2 m) off the ground on Pender Island in British Columbia, Canada, thinks at least. The house, used as a vacation home for the owner, is built on a platform and supported with a pole and attached to a cedar tree. Nicknamed "Raven Loft," the main living area has a toilet and sink, but no shower.

HOUSE ON WHEELS

SIZE: 188 square feet (17.5 sq m)
LOCATION: Anywhere! This house is portable.
CRAZY-SMALL FEATURE: A two-in-one washer-dryer

This little house, called the Cypress, can fit in just about any little nook—because it has wheels to get it there! It's attached to a trailer and able to be towed by a pickup truck. The Cypress may be portable, but it checks many of the boxes of a regular home, including space for a king-size bed in the loft, a two-burner stovetop, and an air conditioner.

SMALL, SPARKLY, AND EXPENSIVE!

A one-carat gemstone weighs a mere .007 ounce (200 mg), but it can be worth a small fortune. Check out these valuable gemstones that shine bright.

DIAMOND

Diamonds may not be the most expensive gemstone—they can cost "only" $15,000 per carat—but they are easily the most recognizable. Composed of pure carbon, diamonds are usually formed more than 90 miles (150 km) under the surface of Earth, where it is hot and there is high pressure—two key components for the formation of diamonds. Taking at least one billion years to form, diamonds make their way closer to the surface during deep volcanic eruptions.

TAAFFEITE

Taaffeite (pronounced TAR-fight) is a rare gemstone that has only been found in two countries: Sri Lanka and Tanzania. Usually reddish or purplish in color, it was first identified in 1945 and comes with a hefty price tag. At $35,000 per carat, you might want to start saving your pennies now!

GRANDIDIERITE

The rare greenish-blue grandidierite gem was first discovered on the island of Madagascar more than 100 years ago. Compared with taaffeite, it's a bargain at only $20,000 per carat! Unless, of course, you want transparent grandidierite, which is the most sought after and even more difficult to come by.

RED DIAMOND

Red diamonds are the rarest color—there have only ever been a few dozen found. Belonging to that kind of exclusive club comes at a price—about $1 million per carat—which means red diamonds are among the most expensive gemstones money can buy.

SERENDIBITE

Serendibite gets its name from *Serendib*, the Arabic name for Sri Lanka, where the mineral was discovered. At one time it was among the rarest gems in the world, with only a few specimens in existence. But when more were found in Myanmar in 2005, it slightly lowered its exclusive status— and its worth, to about $18,000 per carat.

PETITE PARKS

In the category of smallest, these recreation spots hit it out of the park!

MINI CENTRAL PARK

OASIS CRUISE SHIP

A miniature version of New York's Central Park sometimes floats in the middle of the Caribbean Sea. (OK, to be a little more specific, the park is on a cruise ship that sails on the Caribbean.) The living garden, called Central Park, is found on some Royal Caribbean ships and includes trees reaching two and a half decks high, vines, ferns, shrubs, and tropical flowers. Whereas the real Central Park is 2.5 miles (4 km) long, this Central Park is only about the length of two Olympic-size swimming pools.

SMALLEST PARK IN THE BIG APPLE

LUKE J. LANG SQUARE

Contrary to its name, the smallest park in New York City, Luke J. Lang Square, is actually a triangle. Measuring 1/1000 of an acre (.0004 ha), the park honors World War I soldier Luke J. Lang, who lived in a nearby neighborhood. The park is filled almost entirely with hedges, but to get a sense of the size, only 40 people lined up shoulder-to-shoulder could squish in this space!

SMALLEST
NATIONAL PARK

HOT SPRINGS NATIONAL PARK

The smallest national park in the United States was also one of the first. Established in 1921, Hot Springs National Park, located in Arkansas, is just 5,500 acres (2,226 ha), but it contains 47 mineral springs that spout a million gallons (3.8 million L) of 143°F (62°C) thermal water. Visitors are no longer allowed to go for a swim, but they can drink some of the fresh spring water at special fountains located around the park.

WORLD'S SMALLEST **PARK**

MILLS END PARK

Up for a walk in the park? That will be more like one stride at Mills End Park in Portland, Oregon, U.S.A. At just two feet (0.6 m) wide, about as big as a car tire, Mills End is considered the world's smallest park. Once a hole in the middle of a street where a light pole was going to be placed, a journalist planted flowers there in 1946 and it officially became a city park 30 years later. Over the years, people have made additions to Mills End, decorating it with everything from a mini Ferris wheel to flying saucers.

SAVE OUR PARK

ALL EARS

Fennec foxes may be the smallest of all species of fox, but what they lack in size they make up for in ... ears! Measuring up to six inches (15 cm) long, those enormous sound-scanners actually serve as built-in AC units. In the Sahara (and other areas of North Africa where these animals live), daytime temperatures can soar to more than 130°F (54°C). Fennec foxes beat the heat by burrowing up to three feet (0.9 m) in the sand and letting their oversize ears (which are covered in tiny blood vessels) radiate their body heat. At night, when temperatures dip below 55°F (13°C), these nocturnal cuties rely on their thick, insulated coats to keep warm as they hunt for plants, insects, and reptiles to snack on.

FENNEC FOXES HAVE **HAIRY FEET** THAT PROTECT THEM FROM THE **HOT DESERT SAND.**

MINI IS MIGHTY

Who're you calling little? In this smackdown, the tiniest one rules!

SMALLEST APPLE VS. SMALLEST ORANGE

WINNER

It turns out you *can* compare apples to oranges. Tiddly Pommes, grown in New Zealand, are about the size of a golf ball and are considered the world's smallest apple. But this two-bite fruit is just a smidge larger than the clementiny, a 1.5-inch (4-cm)-diameter citrus fruit that is native to China and about a third the size of a clementine.

ROBOBEE VS. BUMBLEBEE

Be careful not to take a swat at this buzzing bot! About half the length of a paper clip and inspired by the biology of a bee, the RoboBee was invented by Harvard researchers as a robot that could one day help with pollinating crops. Bumblebees are about the same size, but of course they've had the pollinating thing down for ages. And no tether required.

TIE

WINNER

SMALLEST ANTELOPE vs. SMALLEST PENGUIN

This one seems like a no brainer—*surely* the smallest species of antelope stands taller than the smallest species of penguin ... right? Think again! Little blue penguins, which are native to Australia and New Zealand, measure up to a whopping average height of 12 inches (30 cm), but the royal antelope, found in the rain forests of West Africa, stands just 10 inches (25 cm) tall! That's the size of a toaster!

SHORTEST U.S. PRESIDENT vs. SHORTEST NBA PLAYER

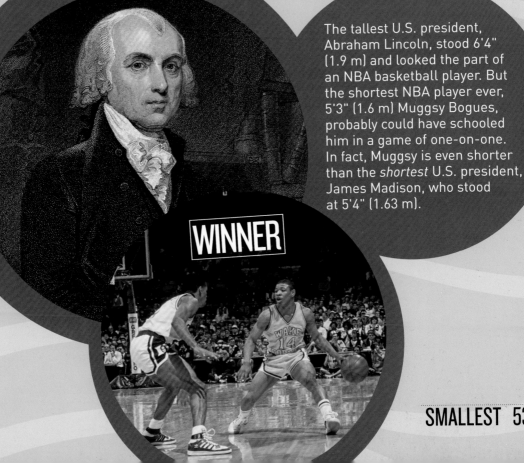

The tallest U.S. president, Abraham Lincoln, stood 6'4" (1.9 m) and looked the part of an NBA basketball player. But the shortest NBA player ever, 5'3" (1.6 m) Muggsy Bogues, probably could have schooled him in a game of one-on-one. In fact, Muggsy is even shorter than the *shortest* U.S. president, James Madison, who stood at 5'4" (1.63 m).

WINNER

IS THERE A BOOK CALLING YOUR NAME?

Then you might want to visit London's Lewisham Micro Library! Set up by a local resident as a "free literary resource," the entire library fits inside a signature red phone booth. Bookshelves, which replaced the old telephone, are filled with titles for all ages.

OPEN 24 HOURS

AMOUNT PAID FOR THE PHONE BOOTH $1.25

WIDTH 3.3 FEET (1 M)

SHELVES 8

HEIGHT
9 FEET
(2.7 M)

COST TO
RENOVATE THE
BOOTH INTO A
LIBRARY
$600

COST TO
BORROW A
BOOK
$0

TOTAL
BOOKS
200

BITTY BIRDS AT A GLANCE

1 SMALLEST HUMMINGBIRD

The bee hummingbird is not only the smallest hummingbird—it's also the world's smallest bird! These tiny residents of Cuba are able to fly at speeds of up to 30 miles an hour (48 km/h) and can move straight up, down, backward—even upside down! Females lay eggs the size of a pea in nests made of moss and spiderwebs.

2 SMALLEST OWL

The name of the world's smallest owl is a bit of a giveaway. About the size of a sparrow, the elf owl hunts insects and other invertebrates at night, snatching them in its feet. Elf owls live in the deserts and wooded canyons of Mexico and the southwestern U.S.

3 SMALLEST RAPTOR

Don't underestimate the strength of the world's smallest raptor. The black-thighed falconet, found in Southeast Asia, is only about 5.9 inches (15 cm) and feasts mostly on invertebrates but will eat another small bird when given the chance!

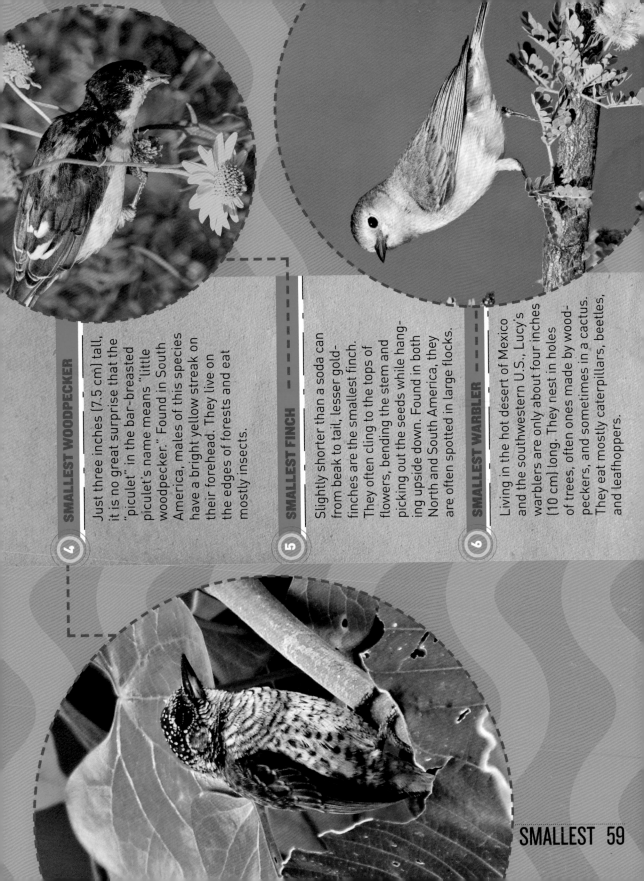

4 SMALLEST WOODPECKER

Just three inches (7.5 cm) tall, it is no great surprise that the "piculet" in the bar-breasted piculet's name means "little woodpecker." Found in South America, males of this species have a bright yellow streak on their forehead. They live on the edges of forests and eat mostly insects.

5 SMALLEST FINCH

Slightly shorter than a soda can from beak to tail, lesser gold-finches are the smallest finch. They often cling to the tops of flowers, bending the stem and picking out the seeds while hanging upside down. Found in both North and South America, they are often spotted in large flocks.

6 SMALLEST WARBLER

Living in the hot desert of Mexico and the southwestern U.S., Lucy's warblers are only about four inches (10 cm) long. They nest in holes of trees, often ones made by wood-peckers, and sometimes in a cactus. They eat mostly caterpillars, beetles, and leafhoppers.

WORLD'S SMALLEST (PRODUCTION) CAR

No problem getting into a parking spot with this car! The Peel P50, considered the smallest car in production, is just 4.5 feet (1.4 m) long. That's about a third the length of a Mini Cooper! It has three wheels, one door, and one seat. The first Peel was made in 1962 and was designed as a commuter car, carrying one person plus a briefcase. Today's Peel P50 buzzes around the streets of Britain (where it is made) at speeds up to 28 miles an hour (45 km/h).

THE PEEL **P50** HAS ONLY **ONE HEADLIGHT.**

READY FOR A MINI MATCHUP?

MATCH EACH OBJECT TO ITS COUNTERPART OF EQUAL SIZE.

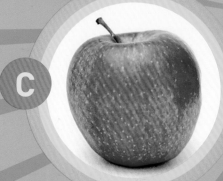

A

B

C

D

1

2

3

4

E

F

5

6

CHAPTER 3

START YOUR ENGINES!
THIS BOOK IS ABOUT TO GO INTO OVERDRIVE AS WE CATCH UP WITH THE FASTEST THINGS IN THE WORLD.

Don't blink! The speediest stuff on the planet might just pass you by. From rocket ships to race cars to high-speed elevators, discover the world's fastest feats—before they're gone in a flash!

USAIN BOLT

Faster than the speed of lightning (or so it seems!), his name says it all: Usain Bolt holds the world record for the 100-meter and 200-meter track sprints. He's so fast that in 2016, the 6'5" (1.96-m) Jamaican track star also completed a "triple-triple," earning three gold medals at each of three consecutive Olympic Games. Bolt may have bolted to the front of the pack, but he wasn't an overnight sensation. He began winning big track races when he was 14, starting out as a hurdler, not a sprinter. He also competed in the high jump and played cricket. The world's fastest human, who retired from competing in 2017, is also famous for the "Lightning Bolt," a signature move of bending one elbow and straightening the other at an angle toward the sky.

NAME:
USAIN BOLT

NATIONALITY:
JAMAICAN

HEIGHT: **6'5"
(1.96 M)**

SHOE SIZE: **13**

NUMBER OF OLYMPIC GOLD MEDALS: **NINE**

TOP RUNNING SPEED: **27.8 MPH (44.7 KM/H)**

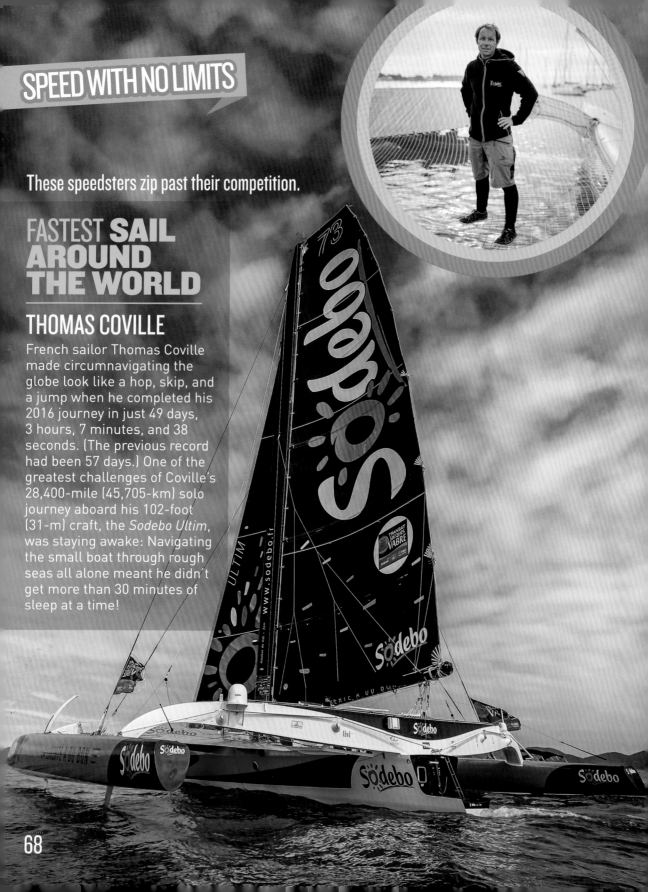

SPEED WITH NO LIMITS

These speedsters zip past their competition.

FASTEST SAIL AROUND THE WORLD

THOMAS COVILLE

French sailor Thomas Coville made circumnavigating the globe look like a hop, skip, and a jump when he completed his 2016 journey in just 49 days, 3 hours, 7 minutes, and 38 seconds. (The previous record had been 57 days.) One of the greatest challenges of Coville's 28,400-mile (45,705-km) solo journey aboard his 102-foot (31-m) craft, the *Sodebo Ultim*, was staying awake: Navigating the small boat through rough seas all alone meant he didn't get more than 30 minutes of sleep at a time!

FASTEST **GROWING PLANT**

BAMBOO

Here's a plant you can actually see growing right before your eyes! Bamboo, the world's fastest growing plant, can grow up to about three feet (0.9 m) in a single day. This fantastic flora has some pretty sturdy roots—an expansive underground network of stems that store and share energy, allowing them to sprout up efficiently.

FASTEST **SPEEDWAY**

BONNEVILLE SALT FLATS

When car and motorcycle racers have a need for speed, there's one place they go to set the record straight: Bonneville Salt Flats. Located in northwest Utah, U.S.A., the salt flats formed after a huge lake dried at the end of the last ice age about 12,000 years ago, leaving behind an expanse of salt that's ideal for drivers to race on. The flats are hard-packed, smooth, flat, and there are no obstacles in the way. And there is no speed limit on the speedway—some rocket-powered vehicles have hit speeds of more than 600 miles an hour (966 km/h)!

FASTEST **SPACECRAFT LAUNCH**

NEW HORIZONS

3-2-1 ... blast off! Rocketing from Cape Canaveral, Florida, U.S.A., in 2006, the New Horizons spacecraft sped away from Earth at more than 35,000 miles an hour (56,327 km/h)—faster than any other spacecraft in history. Thirteen months later, it zipped right by Jupiter, snapping pics and sending them back to Earth along the way; in 2015, it performed a six-month flyby of Pluto and its moons. Settling into a cruising speed of 32,000 miles an hour (51,499 km/h), New Horizons is now hundreds of millions of miles beyond Pluto and more than 3.5 billion miles (5.6 billion km) from Earth.

UP, DOWN, ROUND, AND ROUND

Traveling fast in every direction.

FASTEST **WINGBEAT**

RUBY-THROATED HUMMINGBIRDS

When ruby-throated hummingbirds are in flight, their wings are all a blur! That's because the members of this species are known for their super-swift flapping—up to 53 times per second—which causes their namesake humming sound. These hummingbirds fly with precision and are able to stop in an instant and even hang in midair. Unlike most birds that flap their wings, hummingbirds can rotate their wings, allowing them to fly up, down, sideways—even backward.

FASTEST **TORNADO**

OKLAHOMA CITY

This record will make your head spin! The world's fastest wind speed generated by a tornado was 318 miles an hour (512 km/h), recorded outside of Oklahoma City, Oklahoma, U.S.A., in 1999. That speed is the highest level of a category F-5 tornado, which can cause houses to come off their foundations and trees to be pulled from their roots. Now that's a furious funnel!

FASTEST DELIVERY SYSTEM
YOUR BRAIN

Think email is the fastest way to send a message? Well, get this—there's something even faster ... and it's right inside your own head! That's right, it's your brain. That squishy lump of gray matter in your noggin can send a message faster than you can say "go." Messages sent along neurons, specialized cells designed to send signals to other cells within the nervous system, travel as fast as 268 miles an hour (431 km/h). That's as quick as Formula One race cars at top speed!

FASTEST ELEVATOR
SHANGHAI TOWER

Hold on to your hat! To carry passengers to the observation deck on the 119th floor, 1,841 feet (561 m) from ground level, elevators at Shanghai Tower, in Shanghai, China, reach a top speed of 45.8 miles an hour (73.8 km/h) during the 55-second ride.

MEASURING THE SPEED OF LIGHT

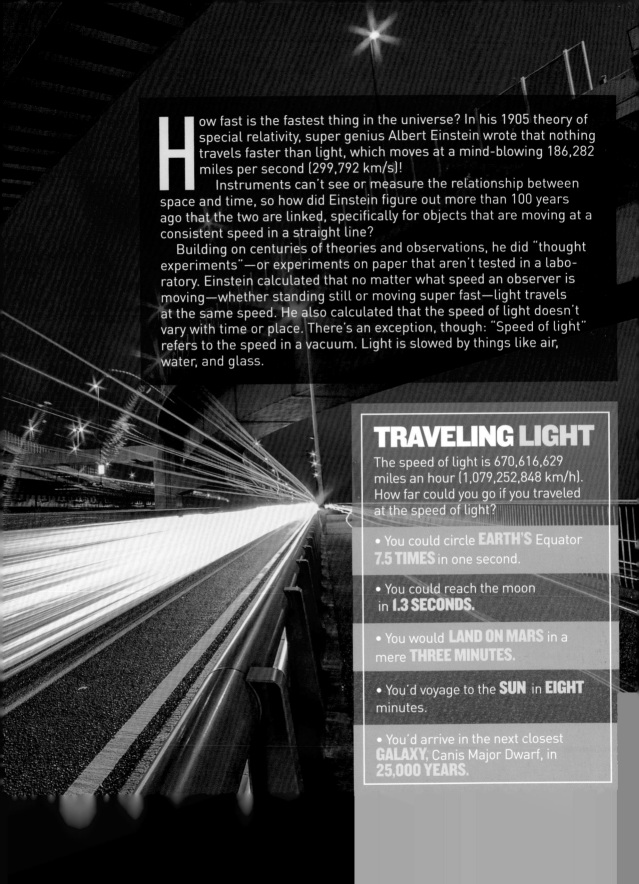

How fast is the fastest thing in the universe? In his 1905 theory of special relativity, super genius Albert Einstein wrote that nothing travels faster than light, which moves at a mind-blowing 186,282 miles per second (299,792 km/s)!

Instruments can't see or measure the relationship between space and time, so how did Einstein figure out more than 100 years ago that the two are linked, specifically for objects that are moving at a consistent speed in a straight line?

Building on centuries of theories and observations, he did "thought experiments"—or experiments on paper that aren't tested in a laboratory. Einstein calculated that no matter what speed an observer is moving—whether standing still or moving super fast—light travels at the same speed. He also calculated that the speed of light doesn't vary with time or place. There's an exception, though: "Speed of light" refers to the speed in a vacuum. Light is slowed by things like air, water, and glass.

TRAVELING LIGHT

The speed of light is 670,616,629 miles an hour (1,079,252,848 km/h). How far could you go if you traveled at the speed of light?

- You could circle **EARTH'S** Equator **7.5 TIMES** in one second.

- You could reach the moon in **1.3 SECONDS.**

- You would **LAND ON MARS** in a mere **THREE MINUTES.**

- You'd voyage to the **SUN** in **EIGHT** minutes.

- You'd arrive in the next closest **GALAXY,** Canis Major Dwarf, in **25,000 YEARS.**

FAST FOOD

There's no such thing as table manners at these food competitions! The person who can clean their plate the fastest is the culinary champ of quick cuisine.

CHICKEN NUGGETS

No time for dipping sauce: Sonya Thomas, of Virginia, U.S.A., once ate 80 chicken nuggets in five minutes. The contest was held during halftime at a New York Liberty women's professional basketball game at Madison Square Garden in 2004.

PIES

Keep your eye on the pie! Martin Appleton-Clare won the Wigan World Pie Eating Championship competition in 2015 by gobbling up steak and kidney pie in just 38.2 seconds. Appleton-Clare, who had also won the title in 2012, went on to be king of the crust again in 2016.

BACON

Mmmm ... bacon. But *182 slices* of bacon gobbled up in five minutes? That's what Matt Stonie did in 2015 to set the bacon-eating world record in Daytona, Florida, U.S.A.

HOT DOGS

Joey Chestnut didn't get the nickname "Jaws" because he savors every bite. He holds dozens of eating competition titles and in 2017 chomped 72 dogs (including the buns!) in 10 minutes during Nathan's Famous International Hot Dog Eating Contest in Coney Island, New York, U.S.A.

PRETZELS

Here's a twist on your typical food-eating competition: Joey Chestnut ate 21 soft pretzels in 10 minutes at a contest in Florida, U.S.A. Not only did he get to claim the title of fastest pretzel-eater, he took home $1,500.

JAPAN'S MAGLEV PROTOTYPE

Japan currently holds the title for fastest passenger train. A prototype maglev (short for magnetic levitation) train, which uses electrically charged magnets to lift the train and move it along the rails (see sidebar on page 77), reached speeds of 374 miles an hour (603 km/h) in a test run. The plan is to use the train for service between the cities of Tokyo and Nagoya by 2027. The 174-mile (280-km) journey would be whittled down to 40 minutes, less than half the time it takes now!

FULL STEAM AHEAD

It's a bird! It's a plane! It's a superfast train! The world's quickest trains don't chug along—they whiz by before you can even hear them coming.

AGV ITALO

Better have your camera ready if you want to snag a shot of Italy's high-speed Frecciarossa 1000 train: As soon as you see it coming, it will be thundering past. *Ciao!* The Frecciarossa 1000 regularly speeds through Italy at speeds up to 249 miles an hour (400 km/h) and is the fastest train in Europe. It's more efficient than most other electric trains around the world and is made almost entirely from recyclable materials.

SHANGHAI MAGLEV TRAIN

Currently the fastest commercially operated train, this maglev train runs between Shanghai and an airport 19 miles (30 km) away at a top speed of 267 miles an hour (430 km/h). A mere eight-minute ride, the train is mostly seen as a prototype for fast trains that will soon be running in China.

HOW MAGLEV TRAINS WORK

A maglev train uses electrically charged magnets to lift the train and move it along the rails. Like ordinary magnets, the superconducting magnets used in maglev trains repel one another when matching poles face each other. To make superconducting magnets, magnets are cooled to less than -450°F (-268°C), which generates stronger magnetic fields than regular electromagnets. The magnet fields interact with metal loops that are in the guideway of the train, creating an electric current. Since the train floats, there is little turbulence, making for a smooth ride.

HARMONY CRH380A

Also in China, you can find the Harmony CRH380A, a non-maglev train that cruises at 236 miles an hour (380 km/h) on traditional steel rails. It gets its speed from a powerful engine and because the body of the train is lighter: It's made from plastics reinforced with carbon fibers.

DRAGONFLIES:
MASTERS OF FLIGHT

Soaring up to 35 miles an hour (56 km/h), dragonflies clock the fastest flight speed of any insect. But that's just the beginning of their flight skills: They can decelerate from 35 to zero miles an hour (56 to 0 km/h) in less than a second *and* they can fly backward, sideways ... you name it! Dragonflies have two sets of wings—measuring up to six inches (16 cm) wide—and they are each separately controlled, giving them exceptional maneuverability. To fly effectively, dragonflies' wing muscles must be warm, so they either whirl their wings to warm them up or bask in the sun. Their speed makes them successful hunters, able to nab prey up to 60 percent of their own body weight. Dragonflies' success rate at catching other insects is as high as 95 percent!

These mad flying skills are an inspiration to scientists, who have modeled flying robots after them. One company even made a 17-inch (43-cm)-long drone that looks like a dragonfly and flies in a similar manner. It's controlled by a smartphone, and its four wings beat up to 20 times per second.

DRAGONFLY ANCESTORS THAT LIVED **250 MILLION YEARS AGO** HAD A WINGSPAN OF MORE THAN TWO FEET (0.6 M)!

DRAGONFLIES' **BULGING EYES** GIVE THEM ALMOST 360-DEGREE VISION.

SPEED DEMON SCUFFLE

The race is on! Find out which one in these snappy sets will reach the finish line first in this battle of the swiftest.

Catch some air! Snowboarders may have style on the slopes, but skiers are faster. The top speed for a downhill skier is 158.4 miles an hour (255 km/h). The fastest person ever recorded on a snowboard flew down a mountain at "only" 126 miles an hour (203 km/h).

WINNER

SNOWBOARDER vs. DOWNHILL SKIER

FINGERNAILS vs. TOENAILS

Find yourself clipping your fingernails more often than your toenails? That's because they grow faster—three to four times faster, in fact. Scientists aren't entirely sure why, but one theory is that our fingernails get more wear and tear because of higher use and our bodies respond by increasing their growth rate.

WINNER

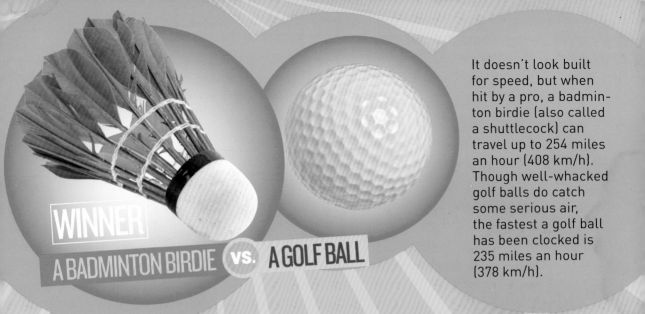

WINNER

A BADMINTON BIRDIE **VS.** A GOLF BALL

It doesn't look built for speed, but when hit by a pro, a badminton birdie (also called a shuttlecock) can travel up to 254 miles an hour (408 km/h). Though well-whacked golf balls do catch some serious air, the fastest a golf ball has been clocked is 235 miles an hour (378 km/h).

WINNER

GREAT WHITE SHARK **VS.** BOTTLENOSE DOLPHIN

Bottlenose dolphins cut through ocean waters with ease and grace, but these sleek mammals come in second to one of the most famous fish in the sea: Great white sharks have them beat, reaching speeds up to 25 miles an hour (40 km/h). Dolphins can reach 22 miles an hour (35 km/h). Not only are these sharks fast, they can also go the distance: Researchers tracked one great white that traveled round-trip between Africa and Australia—a total of 12,400 miles (19,956 km) over nine months!

CIRCLING THE INDY 500

The Indy 500, held annually at the Indianapolis Motor Speedway in Indianapolis, Indiana, U.S.A., offers some pretty sweet and speedy stats.

500 miles (805 km): Total distance of the race

2.5 miles (4 km): Distance of one lap around the track

47 years, 360 days: Age of the oldest winner of the Indy 500

1911:
Year of the first Indy 500

8 seconds:
Average time it takes a pit crew to change four tires and add fuel to a race car

37.895 seconds:
FASTEST OFFICIAL SINGLE LAP

105°F (41°C):
Average temperature in the cockpit of the race cars

22 years, 80 days:
Age of youngest winner of the Indy 500

4Gs:
Force withstood by drivers on turns

"FAST" WAS SLOW IN THE OLD DAYS

A quick look back at the early days of transportation

In 1886, the first automobile looked more like a horse-drawn carriage than a car. Invented by German Karl Benz, it was powered by a .75-horsepower one-cylinder engine and fueled by gasoline. It had three wheels, seated two, and lacked a roof or doors and plodded along at a modest 10 miles an hour (16 km/h)—about as fast as a horse-drawn carriage, actually!

Traveling by air wasn't much faster when airplanes were first invented. Once the Wright Brothers found the winning formula to get their aircraft—the Wright Flyer—off the ground in 1903, they flew as fast as 34 miles an hour (55 km/h) over 852 feet (260 m). Their goal was to achieve flight (without crashing); they weren't worried about how fast they were going once they were airborne.

The first bicycle was fast if you were going downhill—the steeper the slope the faster the speed—but it had a little problem with stopping: It didn't have brakes! And it didn't have any pedals either. Baron Karl von Drais de Sauerbrun of Germany invented a two-wheeled bicycle in 1817 with a seat and handlebars; you made it go by pushing off with your feet, and you stopped it with your feet too!

ASTRONAUT NEIL ARMSTRONG TOOK A PIECE OF **FABRIC** FROM THE **LEFT WING** OF THE 1903 WRIGHT FLYER ON HIS 1969 MISSION TO THE **MOON.**

FAST TRANSPORTATION: THEN AND NOW

THEN: First car (1886): 10 miles an hour (16 km/h)
NOW: Fastest production car: 140 miles an hour (225 km/h) (Dodge Demon)

THEN: First powered-plane flight (1903): 34 miles an hour (55 km/h)
NOW: Fastest manned aircraft: North American X-15: 5,110 miles an hour (8,224 km/h)

THEN: First motorcycle (1885): 7 miles an hour (11 km/h)
NOW: Fastest motorcycle: 376 miles an hour (605 km/h)

THEN: First bicycle (1817): Speed varied depending on terrain
NOW: A recumbent bicycle in Holland reached speeds of 83 miles an hour (133 km/h)

FAST AT A GLANCE

① FASTEST SPINNING PLANET

Not only is Jupiter the largest planet in the solar system, it also rotates the fastest in our solar system—about once every 10 hours. (By comparison, Earth completes one rotation every 24 hours.) At its equator, Jupiter rotates at a speed of 28,000 miles an hour (45,062 km/h)!

② FASTEST AVALANCHE

Not all avalanches involve snow. The fastest avalanche ever recorded was the result of the eruption of Washington, U.S.A.'s Mount St. Helens volcano in 1980. It triggered an avalanche of hot ash and debris that reached speeds of 250 miles an hour (402 km/h).

③ FASTEST TECTONIC PLATES

Imagine moving slower than a sloth and still setting world records. The Earth's dozen tectonic plates are always moving, but some are speedier than others. The Pacific, Nazca, and Cocos plates are the fastest, moving about six inches (15 cm) per year, leaving the slowpoke plates—which move as little as one inch (2.5 cm) per year—in their wake.

Greyhounds can do more than cover a lot of ground fast—some even seem to be able to fly through the air: Greyhound Cinderella May once cleared a jump of 5 feet 8 inches (172.7 cm)! These agile pups may trace their ancient origins to dogs depicted in Egyptian tombs around 4000 B.C.

4 FASTEST KNITTER

Imagine how quickly you could make a Christmas sweater if you could knit 118 stitches in one minute! That's how fast Miriam Tegels of the Netherlands can knit when she's put to the test. Her secret: listening to Motown and R&B music, which she says helps her keep her rhythm.

5 FASTEST DOMESTIC CAT

The Egyptian Mau is a serious threat to any house mouse. This domestic cat can run at speeds up to 30 miles an hour (48 km/h)! The spotted kitty has quick reflexes and loose skin, which helps make it more agile.

6 FASTEST DOG

If greyhounds could enter the Olympics, they would clean up the sprint events in track and field. They can reach speeds of 43 miles an hour (69 km/h) without making it look hard. Besides being light-footed, greyhounds are known for being gentle.

THE BRANCHES THAT **GROW** ON **AXOLOTLS' HEADS** ARE ACTUALLY **GILLS.**

RAPID REGROWTH

The Mexican axolotl (pronounced ACK-suh-LAH-tuhl) may look more fantastical than fantastic, but these cute little critters are amazing in a very real way: They are remarkably fast at regrowing their own body parts. It takes a little more than a month for an axolotl to regrow a leg and a few weeks to regrow a foot—six times faster than most amphibians. And though it's true that many animals can regenerate lost body parts, like a tail or a limb, Mexican axolotls take it to the next level: They can also regenerate their jaw, and even portions of their spine and brain without any scarring! They also can regrow the *same* limb dozens of times.

Amazingly, an axolotl can receive an organ transplant from another axolotl without ever rejecting it. Scientists are studying the amphibians to see if they can one day replicate this success in people, perhaps helping those suffering from severe burns or loss of limbs.

THE AXOLOTL LIVES EXCLUSIVELY IN A NETWORK OF LAKES AND CHANNELS NEAR MEXICO CITY, MEXICO, AND ALMOST NEVER LEAVES THE WATER.

MYTH-BUSTING!

Test your knowledge on all things speedy in this true-or-false myth-busting pop quiz.

TRUE **OR** FALSE ?

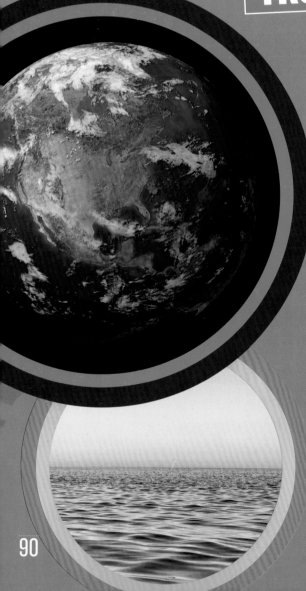

MYTH:
The Earth would spin faster if the moon weren't orbiting it.

TRUE OR FALSE? **TRUE!**
No full moons? No "once in a blue moon?" Things would be a lot different if the moon weren't circling Earth, including the fact that Earth would be spinning much faster than it does now! Without the moon, our day would be only about six hours long. Why? The moon affects Earth's tidal interactions, slowing the Earth way down. A lack of moon would also lead to faster winds and stronger storms.

MYTH: Sound travels through air faster than through water.

TRUE OR FALSE? **FALSE!**
Sound travels through water about four times faster than it travels through air. Because water is denser than air, it takes more energy to *generate* a sound wave in water, but once a wave has started, it will travel faster than it will in air. Case in point: Scientists think humpback whale sounds may travel up to 10,000 miles (16,093 km) through ocean waters!

MYTH: Flying eastbound is faster than flying westbound.

TRUE OR FALSE?
TRUE!

The distance is the same, but time sure does fly when you travel eastbound in the Northern Hemisphere. Why? The jet stream! That's a high-altitude wind that always blows from the west to the east across the Atlantic. Planes traveling east have the wind in their favor.

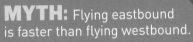

MYTH: Small raindrops fall faster than large ones.

TRUE OR FALSE?

FALSE! (USUALLY)

A large raindrop, one about as big as a housefly, falls at about 20 miles an hour (32 km/h). Small raindrops travel at about two miles an hour (3 km/h). Large raindrops win because they are heavier. There is one exception: Researchers recently discovered that small raindrops that break off from large raindrops fall at the large raindrop's rate, even though they are much smaller, but scientists are unsure why.

CHAPTER 4

BRACE YOURSELF: THINGS ARE ABOUT TO GET WEIRD.

From outdoor oddities to man-made marvels, bizarre beasts to offbeat feats, prepare to behold all of the strange places and faces this planet has to offer. From quirky to curious to downright bizarre, one thing's for sure: You'll never look at the world the same way again!

SALINA TURDA, ROMANIA

This theme park showcases a hidden underground world! Its story begins millions of years ago in a warm, wet sea in what is today Romania, a country in Eastern Europe. Salt deposits hundreds of feet thick were left behind once the sea dried up, and, as time passed, people began to remove the salt for human use. Salt was mined here for hundreds of years, until 1932. When the mine closed, a huge underground cavern as deep as a 40-story building was left in the ground. Today, an unconventional amusement park fills the space. Visitors can ride a 66-foot (20-m)-long Ferris wheel, row a boat on the lake, play table tennis or mini-golf, and even catch a show at a small amphi-theater—all surrounded by massive walls of salt. The subterranean setting makes this theme park one of a kind!

THE **MINE** WAS USED AS AN ANTIAIRCRAFT **BOMB SHELTER** IN WORLD WAR II AND HAS ALSO BEEN USED TO STORE CHEESE.

LOCATION: **TURDA, TRANSYLVANIA, ROMANIA**

DATE OF FIRST MINING OPERATIONS: **1690**

DATE OF MINE CLOSING: **1932**

AMOUNT OF SALT LEFT IN THE MINE:
SOME 38 BILLION TONS (34.5 BILLION T)

DATE THEME PARK OPENED:
JANUARY 2010

ANNUAL VISITORS:
MORE THAN A HALF MILLION PEOPLE

Check out these weird wonders brought to you by Mother Nature!

AURORA **BOREALIS** AND AURORA **AUSTRALIS**

Every night the skies around the North and South Poles erupt in swirling, glowing curtains of color. The aurora borealis (in the north) and the aurora australis (in the south) occur when electrons from the solar wind collide with oxygen and nitrogen gases in the upper atmosphere. These fascinating whirls of color are best seen during the winter, when skies are dark (and of course when they aren't hidden by clouds). Talk about a light show!

BEAVER **DAM**

It took a little help from above to discover this sensational structure. A Canadian researcher reviewing satellite images of Wood Buffalo National Park in Alberta, Canada, noticed something long—very long—from high up in the sky. Turns out it was a beaver dam! Busy beavers build these barriers out of mud, gravel, and sticks to create natural wetlands. In this case, these crafty beavers built a dam that stretches for some 2,800 feet (850 m)—that's about half a mile!

KAWAH IJEN **VOLCANO**

Forget those images of smoking red lava pouring down the side of an erupting volcano: The Kawah Ijen volcano in Indonesia burps blue flames instead! Why so blue? Sulfuric gases seep out from cracks in the volcano at superhigh temperatures—as hot as 1112°F (600°C). When these gases meet the air, they combust into blue flames and can even turn into burning liquid sulfur.

DARVAZA **CRATER**

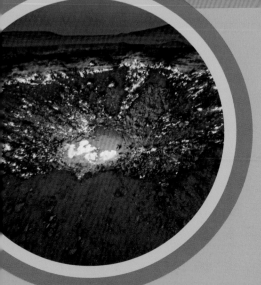

Talk about a slow burn. This natural gas fire pit has been burning for decades in the Karakum Desert of Turkmenistan, a country in central Asia. What happened? In 1971, scientists drilling for oil accidently punctured a pocket of natural gas. Since the seeping gas contained a lot of methane, which can make it hard to breathe, they lit the gas on fire in hopes of burning it all off. That hasn't happened (yet) as the supply of gas is still going strong ... nearly five decades later!

These curiosities will make you do a double take.

CHESS BOXING

Put up your dukes ... and your knights? The sport of chess boxing is the ultimate test of both brains and brawn. Contestants begin with a chess game that is then interrupted by five rounds of boxing that last three minutes each. Competitors can either get checkmate or a knockout to win. You have to watch out for your rooks—*and* your opponent's right hooks!

SKY DINING

Don't look down! Part fine dining, part amusement park, Dinner in the Sky offers adventurous eaters the chance to enjoy a meal suspended 165 feet (50 m) above the ground. This dangling dining experience is available in more than 45 countries. The view beyond your pasta is out of this world—well, almost!

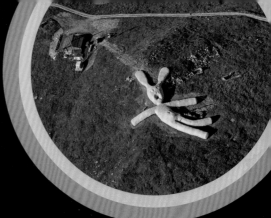

THE **BIG BUNNY**

This stuffed bunny is straight out of a dream—or a nightmare. A group of artists in Vienna, Austria, took five years to knit this giant wool rabbit that lies on a hill in the Piedmont region of Italy, in the Italian Alps. The super-size sculpture is 200 feet (60 m) long and as tall as a two-story building. Hikers come from all over the world to visit the sculpture, named "Hase" or "Hare." You'd better act quick if you want to see this colossal creature, unveiled in 2005: The artists predict that their creation, unsheltered from the elements, will be completely decayed by 2025.

THE **ICEMAN**

Wim Hof isn't just cool, he's ice cold. Hof has made it his mission to see just how much extreme cold his body can withstand, testing his endurance by swimming under ice wearing only swim trunks and by running a half marathon in the snow and ice while barefoot. The Dutch daredevil even climbed Mount Everest—which requires extreme cold-weather gear and clothing—in just a pair of shorts!

SPHERICAL SPECTACLES

Strange spherical stones, some dating back more than 1,000 years, dot the lush rain forest of the Diquís Delta of southwestern Costa Rica. First discovered when workers were clearing the forests to make way for banana plantations in the 1930s, more than three hundred of the fascinating balls have been found so far. The largest ones are more than eight feet (2.4 m) across and weigh 16 tons (14.5 t) (heavier than two African elephants!). But what makes these stones so curious is not just their perfectly round shape—it's that nobody knows exactly how or why the Diquís spheres were made. That mystery has led to a slew of crazy theories about their origins, from alien art to leftovers from the lost continent of Atlantis.

The perfect spheres date back to before Europeans arrived in the Americas, and the civilization that crafted them didn't leave many clues about the purpose of these odd*ball* wonders. But archaeologists suspect that they were created by fracturing and grinding down larger boulders, and that they may have represented political power and social ranking. The stones were unknown for hundreds of years, so just imagine what other surprises might be hiding deep in the world's rain forests!

THE SPHERES REMAINED BURIED UNDER THICK SEDIMENT FOR HUNDREDS OF YEARS.

REPLICAS OF THE SPHERES APPEAR AT THE BEGINNING OF THE MOVIE **RAIDERS OF THE LOST ARK.**

ANCIENT
ODDITIES

If you could travel back in time, you'd see some very different places and faces.

IMMENSE INSECTS
TIME PERIOD: **300 million years ago**

During the history of the Earth, there have been periods of time when oxygen levels in the air were higher than they are now. This abundance of oxygen dramatically increased the size of some insects. A few hundred million years ago, dragonflies had wingspans as large as 2.5 feet (0.8 m)—the width of three Frisbees—and 6-foot (1.8-m)-long mega millipedes were walking around. Talk about your bodacious bugs!

ANTARCTIC PALM TREES
TIME PERIOD: **53 million years ago**

Palm trees ... in Antarctica? Impossible! But pollen samples uncovered by scientists drilling offshore show that it was once indeed the case. Millions of years ago, Antarctica was close to the location where it is today, but temperatures on Earth were warmer. In the summer, it may have even climbed into the upper 70s (degrees Fahrenheit, or about 25 degrees Celsius), which is pretty balmy for the frigid continent.

JUMBO RODENTS
TIME PERIOD: **Eight million years ago**

If you're not a fan of rodents, you might want to skip ahead. *Phoberomys pattersoni*, a now extinct buffalo-size rodent, stretched out to be longer than your family's sofa! The super-charged relative of today's guinea pigs was about four feet (1.2 m) tall and nine feet (2.7 m) long. An almost complete fossil found in Venezuela suggests that it may have tipped the scales at a whopping 1,500 pounds (680 kg).

SIZABLE SEA SCORPIONS
TIME PERIOD: **400 million years ago**

Taking a dip in a German lake during the Devonian period could have brought you face-to-face with a gigantic sea scorpion—that is, if humans had been around back then. But it's probably a good thing we missed it, since the big bug, known as *Jaekelopterus*, had a hard skeleton and could be eight feet (2.5 m) long. Yowza.

PREHISTORIC ELEPHANTS
TIME PERIOD: **14 million years to about 1 million years ago**

This beast may remind you of today's elephant, but this powerful pachyderm was a much different animal. Though *Deinotherium* did live in Africa, like some elephants today, it had a shorter trunk than modern elephants and two-pronged tusks that curved backward (and could be five feet [1.5 m] long!). The ancient land mammal, known as a "hoe-tusker," would also beat today's African elephants in height by a few feet.

VACATION VOYAGES

Is your summer beach outing just not cutting it? Set your sights on these quirky destinations.

SANDSTONE TOWERS
LOCATION: CHINA

The towers of this wild destination look like they belong in a movie—and that may be because they were! Director James Cameron filmed part of the sci-fi movie *Avatar* here, in China's Zhangjiajie National Forest Park. More than 3,000 towers of quartz sandstone reach toward the sky, some more than 650 feet (200 m) tall. Waterfalls, caves, and pools also create this unique, and otherworldly, landscape.

UNDERWATER SCULPTURES
LOCATION: MEXICO

Seeing art through a pair of goggles? Weird! But for visitors to MUSA, or Museo Subacuático de Arte, it's the only way to see the sights. More than 500 sculptures in the museum are submerged in the waters surrounding Cancun, Isla Mujeres, and Punta Nizuc, in Mexico. To really experience the art, visitors should scuba dive through the works. But this museum is not just about art. The sculptures are made of materials that promote the growth of coral life so that the art creates a reef system to support coral and marine animals.

GIANT'S CAUSEWAY
LOCATION: **NORTHERN IRELAND**

This freaky phenomenon of more than 40,000 interlocking basalt columns is pretty strange, but the folklore behind it is even stranger: Once upon a time a giant wanted to cross over to Scotland to teach another giant a lesson, but the water blocked his way. So he threw part of the coast into the sea to create a path. Scientists have another explanation: A volcanic eruption some 60 million years ago created the weird wonder. Either way, rock on!

SOCOTRA ISLAND
LOCATION: **ARABIAN SEA**

Remote Socotra Island, about 220 miles (354 km) off the coast of mainland Yemen, is home to strange plants and animals found nowhere else on Earth. The "dragon's blood" tree, for example—which gets its name from the red resin that flows from its trunk if it's damaged—looks like a gigantic mushroom or a UFO that landed on top of a tree trunk. Socotra has been called the "Galápagos of the Indian Ocean" because of its amazing biodiversity.

IN LIVING COLOR!

Chameleons are truly masters of weird disguises. We know these reptiles are able to change their skin color, but exactly how and why they do this has been a bit of a puzzle. Researchers used to think chameleons did it to camouflage themselves to hide from hungry predators. But scientists studying the clever critters have discovered that their colorful transformations are more often used as a way to communicate with other chameleons. Their skin signals show when they're interested in mating, when they are competing with other chameleons, or even when they're stressed out.

Recently, a team of scientists at the University of Geneva in Switzerland finally figured out how chameleons accomplish this feat. The outer layer of a chameleon's skin is transparent, and below that are special skin cells that contain pigments (substances that cause things to appear certain colors). Below this layer of skin cells, chameleons have another layer that contains super-small (nanoscale) crystals arranged in a triangular pattern. And it is these cells that can be changed to affect how light is reflected, which gives the chameleon the power to change its skin into a kaleidoscope of colors. So in this case beauty really is skin deep!

A CHAMELEON'S TONGUE IS LONGER THAN ITS BODY.

MORE THAN SKIN DEEP
Chameleons have amazing adaptations that help make them powerful predators.

STICKY SPIT Researchers have found that the spit of veiled chameleons is 400 times stickier than human spit. They believe that it's this super stickiness that allows a chameleon to capture prey nearly two-thirds as big as it is.

SUPER VISION A chameleon's eyes can rotate in two different directions at the same time, giving the reptile superb panoramic vision.

TONGUE TIED Snap! Gulp! When a chameleon is hungry for a snack, it unleashes its superfast tongue to snatch up insects like crickets at speeds of 13 miles an hour (21 km/h).

SIZE-ING UP There are more than 200 species of chameleon, some as small as your thumbnail, others as large as a house cat.

WHAT'S

Check out which of these peculiar pairs is crowned the king of kooky.

WEIRDER?

WINNER

A perfume that evoked a stinky English cheese was created to help draw people's attention to blue Stilton cheese, which is made by only a few dairies. But researchers at New York's Bronx Zoo found that some big cats loved the smell of the cologne Obsession for Men and responded by rolling around in it. A scent that can make a wild feline happy is easily the winner!

COLOGNE THAT ATTRACTS BIG CATS **VS.** CHEESE-SCENTED PERFUME

HAIRY FROG **VS.** BASILISK LIZARD

A basilisk lizard uses its fringed rear toes to create a bubble of air that keeps it *on top of the water* as it sprints at speeds of five feet (1.5 m) a second. But that superb skill pales when compared to some frogs in Cameroon, a country in Africa. When threatened, they use a muscle to push claws—which break away from their toe bones—through their toepads. This point goes to the frog!

WINNER

OCTOPUS-FLAVORED ICE CREAM **VS.** TOMATO CANDY

TIE

These treats straddle a thin line between yum and yuck! In Japan, you can lick an octopus-flavored ice-cream cone or suck on a hard candy that tastes like tomato. People flock to buy these Japanese treats! Using unusual and unexpected flavors can produce amazingly tasty results, which in this case means these goodies tie.

"CAT" ISLAND **VS.** "GOAT" TREE

On Aoshima Island in southern Japan, there's a small fishing village where cats outnumber humans. But in Morocco, some goats climb trees to get tasty fruit snacks. What's weirder? The furry felines crowd the dock waiting for tourists to arrive with food, but the goats don't need to rely on humans: They scramble up the thorny argan trees to munch on fruit, even scampering out to the end of branches for a bite! An island full of felines might be *purr*fectly peculiar, but tree-climbing goats win this matchup hooves-down.

WINNER

THE HUMAN BODY

Humans might just be the weirdest thing of all. Check out these supremely strange facts about you!

37.2 trillion
THE NUMBER OF CELLS IN THE HUMAN BODY

10,000 gallons
(37,854 L)
THE AVERAGE AMOUNT OF URINE PRODUCED BY A HUMAN IN A LIFETIME

17,000
THE NUMBER OF TIMES HUMAN EYES BLINK EVERY DAY

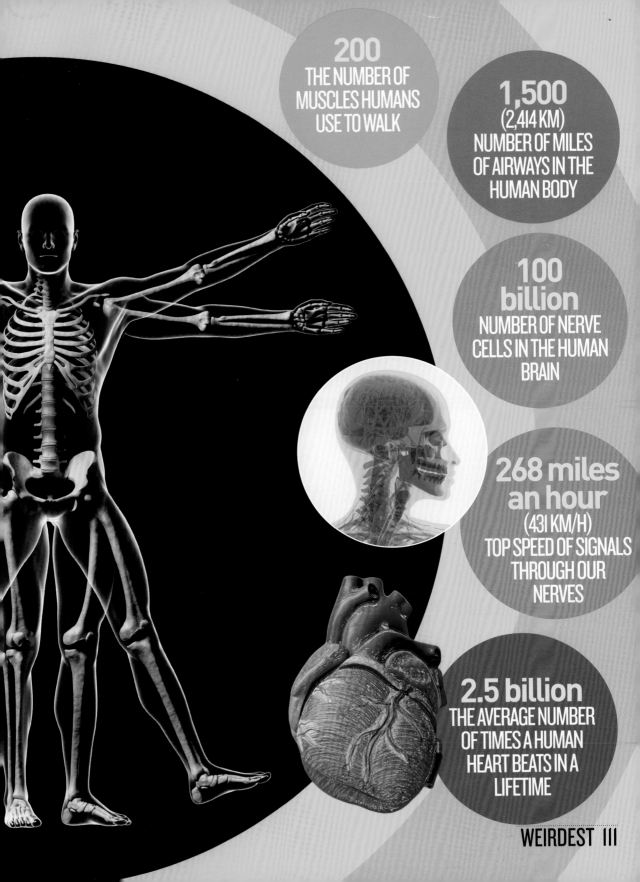

200
THE NUMBER OF MUSCLES HUMANS USE TO WALK

1,500
(2,414 KM)
NUMBER OF MILES OF AIRWAYS IN THE HUMAN BODY

100 billion
NUMBER OF NERVE CELLS IN THE HUMAN BRAIN

268 miles an hour
(431 KM/H)
TOP SPEED OF SIGNALS THROUGH OUR NERVES

2.5 billion
THE AVERAGE NUMBER OF TIMES A HUMAN HEART BEATS IN A LIFETIME

FAR-OUT TECHNOLOGY FROM WAY BACK WHEN

Computers, phones, and even pocket calculators accomplish tasks every day that would have been considered surreal or science fiction just 50 years ago. We've come a long way in a short time, but people have been experimenting with technology for much longer than that. Check out these terrific technological tidbits.

EGYPTIAN SUNDIAL

Before computers, clocks, and apps on smartphones, sundials helped people keep track of the passage of time. It was announced in 2013 that a sundial dating to the 13th century B.C. had been found outside a tomb in Egypt's Valley of the Kings. Scientists think that the flat piece of limestone divided into 12 sections with black lines was used by workers to keep track of the hours they worked. Simple—but important if the workers wanted to get a break.

OSBORNE 1

The first laptop came out in 1981, but it didn't exactly fit comfortably on your lap. The Osborne 1 weighed around 14 pounds (6 kg), which must have given early users a workout. If you had a question about what the portable computer could do, no problem; it also came with a user manual—but that was an additional 777 pages to lug around!

ENIAC

Known as the world's first computer, ENIAC was a beast. The machine took up a whole room and weighed 30 tons (27 t), or about the same as eight large hippos. ENIAC, which stood for Electronic Numerical Integrator and Computer, was finished in 1945, but not in time to be used during World War II to calculate tables for bombing missions (the reason it was created). ENIAC could handle thousands of calculations every second and be programmed to work on different problems. Instead of mechanical parts, ENIAC used nearly 18,000 vacuum tubes.

ANTIKYTHERA MECHANISM

Created by ancient Greeks some 2,000 years ago, the gears and wheels of the Antikythera mechanism were used to tell the phases of the moon, when the sun would rise and set, and even lunar and solar eclipses. But if people hadn't been diving for sponges in the Mediterranean Sea, the bronze pieces of the captivating device may have never been found. The divers discovered the shipwreck containing the Antikythera mechanism in 1900, but it took researchers almost a hundred more years to figure out its real purpose.

WEIRD AT A GLANCE

WEIRDEST PET INSECT

For some pet owners, soothing purrs and happy barks are less appealing than hissing. Appropriately, the Madagascar hissing cockroach gets its name from the sound it makes when exhaling through its breathing holes. These nocturnal insects make their signature sound when fighting or trying to impress a mate. The three-inch (7.5-cm)-long bugs are found on the forest floor of Madagascar, an island off the east coast of Africa, or kept in some people's bedrooms as pets.

WEIRDEST DESSERT

This creamy concoction is only *part* crocodile. An ice-cream parlor in Davao City, in the Philippines, makes its frozen treat using crocodile eggs instead of the usual eggs laid by chickens. This custard is for those sweets-eaters who want a little bite with their ... bites.

WEIRDEST DRINK

Feeling thirsty? This fizzy drink made in India is something to moo about, but you might not want to look too closely at the ingredients: Touted for its healthy properties, gau jal is a cola-like drink made from cow urine.

SINGING DUNES

It's not just the low-pitched rumbling sound that the Eureka Dunes in Death Valley National Park can emit that make them so strangely special. The remote desert dunes are the tallest in California, U.S.A., and the wall of sand rises for more than 680 feet (210 m) into the air. But to hear the sands sing, they have to be bone-dry; any dampness causes the sands to go silent.

4 WEIRDEST ANIMAL

What has fur like a sea otter but lays eggs like a bird? With its mishmash of odd traits, it makes sense that scientists at first thought the duck-billed platypus was a hoax! The Australian animal lacks teeth, so it scoops up insects and other food items from the bottom of rivers, along with mud and gravel, and then mashes it all up in its cheeks. Oh, and males have poisonous spines on their rear feet, which are webbed ... like a duck's.

5 WEIRDEST BUILDING

This house makes visitors feel as if the world has flipped out! Visitors to the Upside Down House in Szymbark, Poland, enter through attic windows and walk around on the ceilings. Built as a statement on how communist rule in Poland upended the country, this is one wacky abode.

6 WEIRDEST PHENOMENON

Dunes that sing? In some places, sand dunes emit a loud, reverberating humming sound when conditions are just right. The low, strange boom originates inside the sand of dunes that are at least 120 feet (37 m) tall, with a slope of over 30 degrees. The weather also must be very, very hot and windy for the serenade to start.

TOTALLY WEIRD SCIENCE

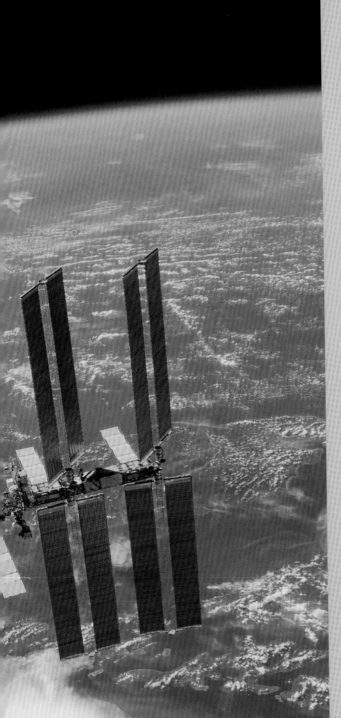

As space explorers dream about watching the sun set on Mars, scientists tackle a more pressing and practical issue: how to make sure there will be enough food and water to sustain us when we make the visit someday to our nearest planetary neighbor. After all, there is no way to order takeout from space (yet!).

One bright idea is to put human waste—in this case, pee—to work in growing nutritious food. Researchers at a lab near Cologne, Germany, are working to reuse urine by having bacteria convert the toxic chemicals found in it into fertilizer that can give plants a healthy boost as they grow. This process removes the ammonia from urine by filtering the liquid through pumice rocks full of bacteria that feed on it, converting it into fertilizer.

It's not as crazy as it sounds! A processing plant on the International Space Station already transforms astronaut sweat, wastewater from washing, and pee into clean, drinkable water. The German researchers plan to launch two greenhouses into space in 2018 to test out their system. Tomato plants will grow in an orbiting garden using a tank of urine, and the setup will mimic conditions on both Mars and our moon. Earthbound researchers will use 16 cameras to watch how the plants fare.

Urine reuse is not only for out-of-this-world applications. Researchers here on Earth are crafting dehydrated foods that can be made into meals by using muddy water or even urine. A semipermeable membrane allows only water to pass through to the food, separating out the good stuff from the yuck. You may never view going to the bathroom the same way again.

A STUDY FOUND THAT ABOUT TWO GALLONS (7.8 L) OF THE LIQUID IN A REGULAR-SIZE BACKYARD POOL IS MADE OF PEE.

WHAT WEIRD DESTINATION IS RIGHT FOR YOU?

Do you like your weirdness from a distance?

Or do you prefer your weirdness up close?

Skylodge Adventure Suites, Calca, Peru

Get cozy in your transparent bedroom capsule 1,000 feet (305 m) up—hanging from the side of a cliff in Peru's Sacred Valley.

Lake Hillier, Middle Island, Western Australia

Researchers think that bacteria in this pink lake give it its rosy color. But since the island is used only for research, your visit will be from the air.

Spotted Lake, British Columbia, Canada

The water of this lake evaporates in the summer, leaving behind small mineral pools of varying color. They're best viewed from far enough away that you can see all the quirky circles at once.

Bonne Terre Mine, Missouri, U.S.A.

Scuba dive to your heart's content in this flooded underground lead mine—now the world's largest freshwater dive resort.

CHAPTER 5

WARNING! DEADLY RECORD BREAKERS ARE LURKING AHEAD.

f you like risky run-ins and foreboding feats, buckle up—this is the chapter for you! But a word of warning: With the turn of each page you'll encounter jeopardizing jobs, perilous predators, lethal locations, pernicious plants, and many more terrible tales. From hidden hazards to pitfalls in plain sight, get ready for a ride into the danger zone.

EARTH-SHAKING SCIENCE

Watch your step! The ground beneath your feet is almost always moving, and those shifts cause earthquakes, tsunamis, and volcanic eruptions to happen all the time. Through the ages, these natural disasters have wreaked havoc around the globe, causing devastating—and deadly—events. So why is Earth so fidgety?

Scientists in the 1960s figured out that the Earth's hard outer layer or crust (known as the lithosphere) isn't a solid mass like the shell of a jawbreaker. Instead, it's divided into moving plates, like a jigsaw puzzle. Heat from our planet's interior circulates very slowly below the lithosphere, causing these plates to move. Where those plates touch at their boundaries, energy is released in the form of volcanoes and earthquakes. Earthquakes happen along fault lines, when the plates slip or slide past one another; magma (that's just lava before it reaches the Earth's surface) can bubble up and lead to a volcanic explosion. When an earthquake happens under the ocean, it can create superlarge waves called tsunamis that race across the ocean and inundate coastal areas. Since plate tectonics is a fact of life, scientists are working hard to predict our planet's next moves.

PERCENT CHANCE OF AN EARTHQUAKE HAPPENING TODAY: **100**

LARGEST EARTHQUAKE ON RECORD: **9.5 ON THE RICHTER SCALE, MAY 22, 1960, AT BÍO-BÍO, CHILE**

LARGEST TSUNAMI WAVE ON RECORD: **1,720 FEET (524 M), JULY 9, 1958, LITUYA BAY, ALASKA**

COUNTRY WITH THE MOST ACTIVE VOLCANOES: **INDONESIA, 45**

NUMBER OF POTENTIALLY ACTIVE VOLCANOES, NOT INCLUDING THE ONES ON THE OCEAN FLOOR: **1,500**

Now accepting applications!

ADVENTURE
PHOTOGRAPHER

Carsten Peter, a National Geographic photographer, plays with fire and ice to help us understand our surprising world. He has gone down to the edge of a superhot lake made of molten rock, climbed into a supercold ice cave on Mount Erebus in frigid Antarctica, and photographed rivers of lava on Italy's Mount Etna. "It's not like I'm actively looking for danger," Peter says. "I want to show people the wonders of nature."

HERPETOLOGIST

One slip in this dangerous job and you could wind up in the hospital. Herpetologists in labs "milk" poisonous snakes by pressing their fangs into a cup to get them to release venom so it can be collected and studied. The venom is used to create antivenom to treat people bitten in the wild or to develop medicines that can be used to help prevent human blood from forming dangerous clots. Now that's *sssseriously sssssuper ssssscience!*

STORM **CHASERS**

To find out what makes tornadoes tick, these gutsy gals and guys head outside when everyone else is heading in. Using armored trucks and special measuring tools, the scientists observe twisters as close as safely possible. They even try and leave scientific instruments (one special one is known as a "turtle" probe) in the tornado's direct path to record its power. This is one twisted job!

UNDERWATER **CAVE DIVERS**

Underwater caves are found all over the world, but there's a lot we don't know about them. They are dark, dangerous, and often hidden, with deep crevasses and secret tunnels. Underwater cave divers explore these submerged lands and can learn about what the climate was like in the past by studying the chemical makeup of cave deposits. They can also discover new cave critters. Some of these unusual organisms may even hold clues about what the earliest creatures were like.

Mother nature's record-setting spots put the "X" in eXtreme!

COLDEST PLACE ON EARTH

ANTARCTICA'S RIDGE A

Calling Antarctica's Ridge A a pretty chill place is a bit of an understatement. The average annual average temperature here is -94°F (-70°C)—cold enough to turn turpentine into a solid block (and that stuff pretty much never freezes!) and any exposed skin into a frostbitten mess. So next time it gets a bit nippy waiting for the school bus, just be thankful you don't live at Ridge A!

HIGHEST POINT ON EARTH

MOUNT EVEREST

Mount Everest is the mother of all mountains: At 29,035 feet (8,850 m) it's the highest point on Earth, making it a destination for super-adventurous and ambitious climbers every year. But it's also one of our planet's most extreme environments: On the summit, winds can gust at over 100 miles an hour (160 km/h) and temperatures get below freezing. Though climbs are usually attempted only when conditions are the mildest, around 300 people have died on the mountain from altitude sickness, accidents, exposure, and avalanches.

DEEPEST POINT ON EARTH

CHALLENGER DEEP

Thousands of people have made it to the highest point on Earth, but only three have ever been to the deepest place on Earth. Humans (and by that we mean professional free divers!) can only explore the ocean a maximum of 400 feet (120 m) down before the immense pressure of the water (and lack of breathable oxygen) starts to compromise their lungs and bodies. To explore deeper, humans had to invent submarines, submersibles, and remotely operated vehicles. Still, only two submersibles (carrying three people total) have ever made it to the deepest known spot on Earth: Challenger Deep in the Mariana Trench, 36,037 feet (10,984 m) below sea level.

HOTTEST PLACE ON EARTH

LUT DESERT

The Lut Desert in southeast Iran is so hot that, until recently, scientists thought it was impossible for animals or plants to live there. Satellite measurements in 2005 found an air temperature of 159.3°F (70.7°C)—the highest ever recorded. The desert is full of sand dunes and wide-open spaces with dark, pebbled ground that is perfect for soaking up the sun's heat. For humans that can be deadly, but that doesn't mean animals can't thrive. Blanford's foxes, reptiles, and spiders all make this scorcher their home.

TINY TERROR

A deadly fungus has been devastating amphibian populations across the world.

When scientists began to notice mysterious frog deaths in the 1980s, they weren't sure of the culprit. In time, they discovered that the amphibians were infected with a chytrid (a type of fungus), which they named *Batrachochytrium dendrobatidis* (Bd). Bd infects a frog's skin, causing it to thicken; this can be deadly because amphibians "drink" water and absorb electrolytes through their skin rather than through their mouths. Unable to transfer vital chemicals through its skin, a frog's heart will stop beating. Not all frogs infected with Bd will die, but for many species it is causing populations to decline and even to go extinct.

Determined researchers are fighting back and trying to save the vulnerable frogs. National Geographic explorer Jonathan Kolby works in Cusuco National Park, in northwestern Honduras. Kolby and his team are focusing their work on three species of tree frogs. By collecting young frogs, curing them from the infection, and then releasing them back into the park as healthy adults, they are giving them a fighting chance. Colonies of healthy frogs will also be kept at a research center in an effort to conserve their croaks for years to come.

TREE FROG, *BOOPHIS PYRRHUS*

NEARLY 4,000 SPECIES OF AMPHIBIANS ARE UNDER THREAT FROM CLIMATE CHANGE, DEFORESTATION, AND Bd.

FANTASTIC FROGS

EXQUISITE SPIKE-THUMB FROG

PLECTROHYLA EXQUISITA
This critically endangered frog breeds in the streams of Cusuco National Park and has been captured for the pet trade. Its body blends into its cloud forest home.

HONDURAS SPIKE-THUMB FROG

PLECTROHYLA DASYPUS
This Cusuco critter used to be common but has lost 80 percent of its population in recent years. It lives at elevations between 4,600 (1,410 m) and 6,500 feet (1,990 m).

COPAN BROOK FROG
DUELLMANOHYLA SORALIA
Loss of habitat in Honduras (and Guatemala) as well as the chytrid fungus have led to declining numbers for this endangered creature. Its striking red eyes and lime green splotches aren't its most unusual feature: The frog's tadpoles swim upside down.

JONATHAN KOLBY

BEAUTIFUL BUT DEADLY:
PERILOUS PLANTS

Some of the world's deadliest things are also some of its loveliest. Oleander's brightly colored flowers make it look harmless and inviting, but beware: Every part of this beautiful plant is poisonous, and it can have devastating effects if you eat it. The plant's toxins can cause severe nausea and dilated pupils—and stop a human heart from beating! Even the sap is toxic, so if it's burning, stay away from the smoke, too. So why is the shrub around? *Nerium oleander* is planted by gardeners because deer and other plant-eaters know its secrets and stay away, protecting the flowers from hungry chompers.

OLEANDER IS THE OFFICIAL **FLOWER** OF HIROSHIMA, JAPAN.

OTHER POISONOUS PLANTS

WHITE SNAKEROOT
AGERATINA ALTISSIMA

This plant caused the death of Abraham Lincoln's mother in 1818, when the future president was only nine years old. Nancy Hanks Lincoln didn't eat the plant but rather drank milk from a cow that had grazed on a field full of the white wildflowers. As settlers expanded into the American West, many didn't know about the dangers of the fragrant snakeroot. The toxins in this plant passed from the cow to its milk, and people who then drank the milk suffered from what was called "milk sickness."

DEADLY NIGHTSHADE
ATROPA BELLADONNA

It's a safe bet that plants with "deadly" in their names usually are not to be messed with. And in the case of this herb, its leaves and berries can all be fatal. Its berries can look like cherries, and because they don't taste terrible, mistaken poisonings can occur. Its roots also pack a powerful punch and have even been used to cause numbness before surgery. Yikes.

WATER HEMLOCK
CICUTA MACULATA

This wildflower grows around wetlands and has small, white flowers and a hollow stem. It can be confused with celery or parsnips, which can lead to dangerous results if eaten, including twitching muscles and stomach pain or convulsions. This is the same plant that Socrates, the ancient Greek philosopher, drank before he died.

PITCHER PLANT
NEPENTHACEAE AND SARRACENIACEAE FAMILIES

The flowers of the pitcher plant are gorgeous but deadly. But it's not humans that must mind this menace—it claims much smaller victims. Insects that get stuck in the plant's "pitcher"—a modified leaf that is filled with a sticky liquid—are toast. Unable to escape, they eventually decompose into plant food. These flowers are not always dainty; they can grow to be three feet (1 m) tall, which is large enough to trap larger prey, such as small frogs.

RECORD-BREAKING CATASTROPHES

These natural disasters wiped out ancient civilizations and reshaped the Earth itself.

SANTORINI VOLCANO ERUPTION

Some 3,600 years ago, a monstrous volcano erupted in the Aegean Sea. The resulting devastation may have wiped out the Minoan civilization and also led to the myth of the lost city of Atlantis. Scientists think that humans have witnessed only one larger eruption, in 1815 in Indonesia.

ANTIOCH EARTHQUAKE

Tens of thousands of people in and around Antioch, in present-day Syria, died in A.D. 526 after a series of devastating earthquakes flattened the city, leading to fires and even more devastation. Antioch, a bustling Roman city at the time, had the misfortune of being located at the edge of a few different tectonic plates, which were prone to abrupt shifts.

CRETE EARTHQUAKE AND TSUNAMI

An earthquake underneath the Mediterranean island of Crete in July, A.D. 365 was so strong that it raised part of the island up by as much as 33 feet (10 m)! But that was just the beginning. As the tsunami wave from the quake raced across the sea, it inundated the Egyptian coastal city of Alexandria, killing tens of thousands of people.

MOUNT MAZAMA

Crater Lake in southern Oregon is no ordinary lake. It was formed by a volcano! When Mount Mazama erupted some 7,700 years ago, the eruption caused the 12,000-foot (3,660-m) volcano to collapse and form the record-breaking lake. The brilliant blue lake is the deepest in the United States and the seventh deepest in the world.

MOUNT VESUVIUS

When smoke started to pour from this volcano on the southwest coast of Italy on the morning of August 24, A.D. 79, the people of Pompeii didn't think they had much to worry about. After all, the mountain had been active before. But this eruption—which lasted for more than 24 hours—included six different waves of toxic gases and rained down hot ash. It killed thousands of people, literally stopping them in their tracks.

BLISTERING BITE

Crocs inspire fear, and for good reason.
Just how powerful are their jaws, anyway?

When scientists set out to measure and compare the bite force of different animals (like lions, tigers, and—of course—crocodiles), they found that saltwater crocodiles were the winners—claws down. (Great white sharks may be slightly stronger, but that hasn't been measured directly—yet!) These death-dealing darlings can bite down with the strongest force of them all—3,700 pounds per square inch (260 kg per sq cm)—compared with lions' and tigers' 1,000 pounds per square inch (70 kg per sq cm). That's about 25 times the force you'd use when chomping down on a piece of pizza!

A saltwater croc has 40 to 60 teeth shaped like ice-cream cones. These teeth are replaced throughout its life, but that's not what makes the bite so fierce. The enormous force comes from the muscles crocs use to close their jaws, not the teeth themselves. In fact, while their superstrength works when they close their jaws, the force doesn't work as well when they open them.

TOOTH TEST

It's easy to tell the difference between crocs and alligators (but we don't recommend getting close enough to check!). With their mouths closed, crocodiles will have two teeth poking up from their lower jaw and over their upper jaw; alligators won't.

A SALTWATER CROCODILE CAN STAY UNDERWATER FOR MORE THAN AN HOUR.

DEADLY MATCHUP

These deadly combos are downright dangerous. Check out which ones on our list are the titans of terror!

WINNER

FUGU vs. RAW EGGS

Fugu is some treacherous sushi! It's made from puffer fish, a creature whose liver, intestines, and ovaries contain enough poison to kill 30 people. Expert chefs can prepare the dish without the toxic parts—but accidents can happen. If raw eggs are not handled and cooked properly, the results can also be dicey—namely, salmonella poisoning—but in most cases it's not fatal.

SHARK vs. SPIDER

Sharks may strike terror in beachgoers, but how often do you see their fearsome fins? Not very often. Spiders, however, seem to be everywhere. Which one is more dangerous? On average in the U.S., sharks cause only about one death a year, but poisonous spiders send seven people to an early grave.

WINNER

TIE

ACKEE FRUIT **VS.** RHUBARB LEAVES

If eaten when not ripe, Jamaica's national fruit, the ackee fruit, can cause severe vomiting and even death. Even its seeds are toxic. Rhubarb stalks are perfectly edible, but its large green leaves contain oxalic acid, which can cause kidney failure if eaten in large amounts (and that can lead to death). This potentially fatal fruit vs. veggie matchup is a tie.

WINNER

HOT AIR BALLOONING **VS.** SKIING AND SNOWBOARDING

Ballooning sends you gently skyward to gaze out over the countryside, while skiing and snowboarding give you a rush of cold air and speed. Both activities are thrilling, but which activity is more dangerous? Over a 12-year-period in the U.S., five people died in balloon crashes. But every year an average of 38 skiers and snowboarders die in accidents.

EPIC EXTINCTIONS

5
NUMBER OF MASS EXTINCTIONS IN EARTH'S HISTORY

95
PERCENTAGE OF MARINE SPECIES THAT DIED OFF DURING A MASS EXTINC- TION SOME 250 MILLION YEARS AGO

70
PERCENTAGE OF LAND SPECIES THAT DIED

65 million
NUMBER OF YEARS AGO T. REX BECAME EXTINCT

3 billion
NUMBER OF PASSENGER PIGEONS IN NORTH AMERICA IN 1800

0
NUMBER OF PASSENGER PIGEONS IN NORTH AMERICA TODAY

739
NUMBER OF EXTINCT SPECIES RECORDED BY SCIENTISTS

50
ESTIMATED PERCENTAGE OF PRIMATE SPECIES NOW THREATENED WITH EXTINCTION

DEADLY NO MORE

People were getting miserably sick and dying in London, England, in 1831. They were plagued with cholera, a disease that causes vomiting, diarrhea, and even death. By the time the epidemic ended the following year, some 50,000 people had died. Scientists believed the disease had been caused by something called "miasmas," or poisonous air.

In September 1848, London suffered another outbreak of cholera. John Snow, a doctor who as a medical apprentice had helped treat patients during the earlier epidemic, studied the affected patients and asked questions about when and where they first became sick. He wrote a small pamphlet that described his idea that cholera was being caused by tainted water, not bad air. But he could not persuade other doctors and scientists.

Cholera returned to London in 1853. Still believing that the disease was waterborne, Snow began comparing the rates of illness in areas of contaminated vs. uncontaminated water. After more than 500 people died in a two-week period in the summer of 1854, Snow's investigating, interviewing the sick, and mapping their locations revealed that most of the people who had become ill had gotten their water from one source. He worked to have the pump handle removed from the well supplying the cholera-infected water, effectively ending the epidemic.

In 1884 a German scientist isolated the bacteria that causes cholera, *Vibrio cholerae.* It can spoil water and food, especially in unsanitary conditions or after a natural disaster when houses and infrastructure have been damaged. Snow was right! His careful studies, mapping, and use of statistics to prove that cholera was waterborne had given rise to epidemiology—the study of diseases and how they spread. Snow is considered the "father" of the field.

OTHER NO-LONGER-DEADLY DISEASES

POLIO
Polio was a devastating disease that could paralyze and even kill its victims; it spread through person-to-person contact, making it extremely dangerous. In April 1954, an American researcher named Dr. Jonas Salk began testing a vaccine he had developed in the hope of preventing infection. Today the polio vaccine is commonplace, although outbreaks still do occur in parts of the world.

TETANUS
Ouch! You've stepped on an old nail. The pain would have been the least of your worries before German researchers invented the tetanus vaccine in the late 19th century. A bacterium found in dust and soil causes tetanus; it enters the body through a break in the skin. Infected people experience "lockjaw," where the muscles of the jaw become hard to open, causing trouble swallowing, breathing, and even death.

SMALLPOX
This disease, spread by the variola virus, caused a skin rash and fever; it once killed about 30 percent of everyone infected. Edward Jenner, an English doctor, introduced the first smallpox vaccine—also the world's first vaccine—in 1796. But it wasn't until 1980 that the World Health Organization declared smallpox finally eradicated.

DR. JOHN SNOW HELPED GREAT BRITAIN'S QUEEN VICTORIA DELIVER HER EIGHTH CHILD, PRINCE LEOPOLD.

DEADLY AT A GLANCE

1. DEADLIEST BOOK

OK—this book isn't actually deadly if you read it. *The Egyptian Book of the Dead* contains spells that the ancient Egyptians believed would help them navigate the afterlife. Now that's some ghostly reading!

2. DEADLIEST MARTIAL ART

What makes the martial art of ninjutsu so deadly is not the kicks and punches, it's the stealth. Ninjutsu is all about spying and guerrilla warfare, not self-defense and combat skills. Ninjutsu practitioners (known as ninjas) used their skills to assassinate rivals starting in feudal Japan more than 300 years ago during a time of political upheaval.

3. DEADLIEST ANIMAL IN THE U.S.

This toxic title goes to some mighty minis: wasps, bees, and hornets. Their stings kill some 58 people a year, mostly as a result of the unlucky victims going into anaphylactic shock (having a severe allergic reaction) after being stung.

EARTH'S TWIN

Venus is the second planet from the sun and the second largest terrestrial planet in our solar system. Its similarity in size and mass to Earth—the largest terrestrial planet in the solar system—has given it the nickname "Earth's twin."

4 DEADLIEST FLOOD

In 1931, a flood hit central China, inundating an area larger than Austria and killing as many as four million people. They didn't all drown; many suffered from the famine and disease that spread after the flood, making this *the* record breaker for natural disasters.

5 DEADLIEST DAY OF THE WEEK

Hats off to Saturdays! Not. The day of the week most associated with chilling out is also the one with the most deaths. To come up with this winner, researchers looked at 39 million deaths in the United States over 15 years. But don't feel bad for the other days of the week; the difference between the day with the fewest deaths (Sunday) and big bad Saturday was less than 2 percent.

6 DEADLIEST PLANET

This is a trick category—we aren't living on other planets so they can't kill us (yet)! But if they could, Venus would win this category hands down. Its superdense atmosphere traps the sun's heat, making it the hottest planet in our solar system, checking in at 880°F (471°C). And the clouds on Venus are made of sulfuric acid. So though you could cook a pizza in seven seconds on Venus, you'd be dead before you could take your first bite.

MARIE CURIE'S LABORATORY NOTES ARE STILL RADIOACTIVE AND MUST BE HANDLED WITH PROTECTIVE GEAR.

MARIE CURIE

Sometimes, groundbreaking work comes at a person's own peril. In the case of renowned scientist Marie Curie, it ultimately led to an early death.

Marie Sklodowska was born in 1867 in Warsaw, Poland, where she lived until she moved to France in 1891 to continue her scientific studies. There, she met her future husband, Pierre Curie, and together they started working to research the invisible rays given off by the element uranium. They knew that a substance called pitchblende, which contained uranium, was very radioactive. But the Curies didn't protect themselves because, at that time, no one understood the lethality of radiation. The Curies would grind up samples and test them repeatedly in their lab. Marie even carried around bottles containing the radioactive elements polonium and radium—which she and Pierre had discovered in their research of pitchblende—in the pocket of her coat!

Pierre was tragically killed in an accident on a Paris street in 1906, but Marie continued with her research. She developed a way to measure radioactivity as well as a mobile x-ray unit that was first used during World War I to assist wounded soldiers. This invention helped determine the location of shrapnel and broken bones, saving lives.

Years of exposure to radioactive materials took their toll on Curie, though, and she died in 1934 at the age of 66. She was awarded two Nobel Prizes for her research, becoming the first woman in the world to receive the prestigious award.

Marie Curie's legacy lives on—not only through the contributions of her scientific breakthroughs but also through her overcoming the barriers she faced as a female scientist. Her hard work and success furthered the goal of women being treated as equals among their male colleagues—and continue to inspire young scientists today.

THE "CURIE" IS A UNIT OF MEASUREMENT FOR RADIOACTIVITY.

IDENTIFY THE LIE

How well do you remember the deadly details in this chapter?
See if you can pick out which of the three facts is actually a fib.

A.

1. Volcanic eruptions can lead to lakes being formed.

2. John Snow discovered radium.

3. A herpetologist "milks" snakes.

B.

1. Japan's national fruit is the ackee fruit.

2. It's cold enough in parts of Antarctic to freeze turpentine into a solid block.

3. Abraham Lincoln's mother died from "milk sickness."

C.

1. An ancient earthquake on Crete raised parts of the island by 33 feet (10 m).

2. Carsten Peter works to save frogs.

3. Clouds on Venus are made of sulfuric acid.

D.

1. Polio causes a terrible skin rash.

2. A saltwater crocodile can remain submerged for more than an hour.

3. Carnivorous pitcher plants can "eat" small frogs.

E.

1. Only three people have been to the deepest part of the ocean.

2. Spider bites are more dangerous than shark ones.

3. There are three billion passenger pigeons on Earth today.

F.

1. Sushi made from puffer fish can be deadly.

2. The largest earthquake in recorded history happened in Alaska.

3. Some 4,000 amphibians are threatened by the chytrid fungus.

ANSWERS: A. 2; B. 1; C. 2; D. 1; E. 3; F. 2

CHAPTER 6

THESE **RAD** RECORD HOLDERS ARE ALL THE UNDISPUTED **COOLEST** IN THEIR CLASS.

From out-of-this-world light shows to hip happenings and sensational scenes, the people, places, and phenomena in this chapter have one thing in common: They take cool to the next level. Which one will be your favorite?

COOLEST 149

BIOLUMINES

MORE THAN **FOUR-FIFTHS** OF BIOLUMINESCENT **CREATURES** LIVE IN THE **OCEAN.**

NUMBER OF SPECIES OF FIREFLIES: **ABOUT 2,000**

COLOR OF LIGHT: **YELLOW, ORANGE, RED, GREEN, BLUE, AND PURPLE**

FIRST RECORDED OBSERVATION: **ARISTOTLE, 350 B.C.**

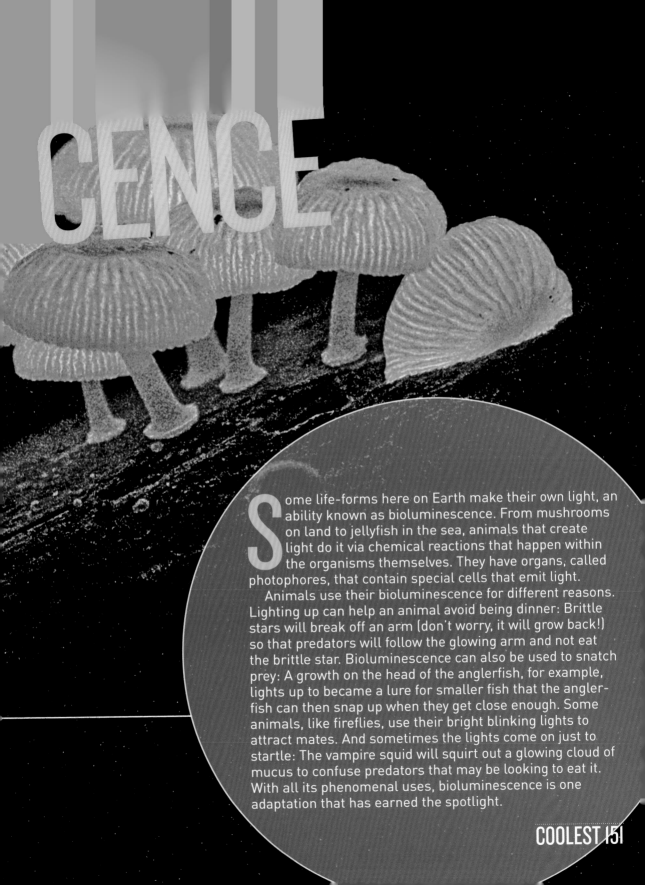

CENCE

Some life-forms here on Earth make their own light, an ability known as bioluminescence. From mushrooms on land to jellyfish in the sea, animals that create light do it via chemical reactions that happen within the organisms themselves. They have organs, called photophores, that contain special cells that emit light.

Animals use their bioluminescence for different reasons. Lighting up can help an animal avoid being dinner: Brittle stars will break off an arm (don't worry, it will grow back!) so that predators will follow the glowing arm and not eat the brittle star. Bioluminescence can also be used to snatch prey: A growth on the head of the anglerfish, for example, lights up to became a lure for smaller fish that the angler-fish can then snap up when they get close enough. Some animals, like fireflies, use their bright blinking lights to attract mates. And sometimes the lights come on just to startle: The vampire squid will squirt out a glowing cloud of mucus to confuse predators that may be looking to eat it. With all its phenomenal uses, bioluminescence is one adaptation that has earned the spotlight.

From itty-bitty insects to colossal clouds, meet some of Mother Nature's coolest creations.

COOLEST THIRSTY INSECT

ANTS

Ants have to drink and eat, just like the rest of us. Most of the time they get the water they need through food, but, on occasion, they go straight to the source: a water droplet. And when photographers take an insect's-eye view of the ants sipping some H_2O, you can eyeball small-scale action that is perman-*ant*-ly cool.

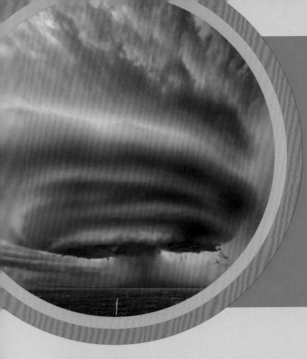

COOLEST CLOUD FORMATIONS

SUPERCELLS

Jaw-dropping supercell clouds—which look a little like giant, puffy flying saucers—are the least common thunderstorm cloud. When supercells form, they can spawn terrible thunderstorms, treacherous tornadoes, wild winds, and harrowing hail. These formations can stretch for several miles and last for hours. Their favorite spots to hang out? The Great Plains of the United States.

COOLEST FEATHERED FOSSIL

DINOSAUR TAIL

The first dinosaur tail found preserved in amber? Cool. If it's covered in feathers? Supercool! About 99 million years ago a dinosaur with a feathered tail became preserved in amber (fossilized tree resin) along with an ant and plant debris. By studying the small wonder unearthed in northern Myanmar, scientists can learn more about the differences in the feathers of birds of flight and dinos like this one, which likely stayed grounded.

COOLEST WINGED FORMATION

STARLING MURMURATION

Mur-mur-what? This fantastic flying phenomenon happens when huge flocks of stocky songbirds called European starlings move in unison. As one bird changes direction, the birds closest to it do the same, leading to a huge dance across the sky. Now that's winging it!

Find out what makes these surprising scenes so astonishing.

COOLEST DIVE

SILFRA CRACK

Did you know you could actually witness continents spreading apart? It's true, but you would have to be pretty patient! The underwater Silfra fissure offers a prime spot for a firsthand look at the dynamics of the tectonic plates that make up the crust of our planet. The crack's location off the coast of western Iceland is along the divide between Europe and North America. While the water is so clear that scuba divers can see for more than 300 feet (100 m), watching the continents spreading apart takes more than clear water: The deep fissure moves apart by only about .75 inch (2 cm) a year.

COOLEST SKATE PARK

ZAP'ADOS

From the outside, this building in Calais, France, looks a little boring; on the inside, it's a whole different story. The former factory space (it was used to roast peanuts) has been turned into a futuristic skate park known as Zap'ados. Daredevils roller blade, skate, and scooter in the middle of more than half an acre (.24 ha) landscape. This place is on a roll!

COOLEST BALANCING ACT

DRINA RIVER HOUSE

Talk about remote. You'll need a canoe and a whole lot of patience to get to this cabin, carefully balanced on a rocky outcrop of the Drina River in the eastern European country of Bosnia and Herzegovina. The far-out abode has been around for more than 40 years, carefully built from materials that were floated over or brought by boat. You can really live on the edge in this cozy cabin!

COOLEST ISLAND FORMATION

SURTSEY

Late in 1963, a cook on board a passing ship saw a column of dark smoke rising from waters off the coast of Iceland. By the following day, an entirely new island was forming in the sea! This wasn't magic though, but rather the work of an erupting underwater volcano. The eruption ended about three and a half years after the cook first saw smoke, and the island, named Surtsey, has been dormant ever since. Researchers have been active, though, studying the volcanic isle to observe what happens when an island is first colonized by plants and animals.

COOLEST 155

IT TAKES **200 MILLION YEARS** FOR THE MILKY WAY TO **ROTATE.**

THE WORLD'S COOLEST LIGHT SHOWS

These four radiant scenes will set your mind aglow.

WHAT: THE MILKY WAY WHERE: THE NIGHT SKY WHEN: EVERY NIGHT CLAIM TO FAME: You don't need to mark your calendar for this incredible light show! Just look to the night sky in an area free of light pollution (artificial light from streetlights and buildings) for a glimpse: That hazy, glowing strip overhead filled with millions of stars is just one of the spiral arms of our home galaxy.

WHAT: YEE PENG WHERE: THAILAND WHEN: NOVEMBER CLAIM TO FAME: In northern Thailand, during the festival of light known as Yee Peng, thousands of lanterns are sent skyward to honor the Buddha and to bring good luck. The event usually happens in November when the moon is full. Candles or small fuel canisters are lit underneath the lanterns to fill them with hot air, after which they are released and rise in unison.

WHAT: FIELD OF LIGHT WHERE: AUSTRALIA WHEN: ONGOING CLAIM TO FAME: Artist Bruce Munro created a field of multicolored lights stretching out toward Uluru, the giant red sandstone outcropping in the heart of the central Australian desert. Some 50,000 bulb lights balance on slender stems and fan out across the desert. Visitors can explore the vivid display, which is the size of seven football fields.

WHAT: KOBE LUMINARIE WHERE: JAPAN WHEN: DECEMBER CLAIM TO FAME: Each December, some 40,000 hand-painted lights create a fantastic scene on a street in Kobe, Japan. Visitors can wander underneath radiant arches of light to soak in the glow. This annual festival began in 1995 as a way to give hope to city residents after the devastating Great Hanshin earthquake damaged the city earlier that year.

COOLEST 157

THE COLD STANDARD

Brrr! A cozy hat and warm gloves might come in handy when reading about these cool winners.

COOLEST LIGHTHOUSE

ST. JOSEPH LIGHTHOUSE, MICHIGAN, U.S.A.

Freezing temperatures and high winds transform a lighthouse on the southern shores of Lake Michigan into an icy wonderland. As waves crash over the lighthouse pier jutting into Lake Michigan, the spray freezes and creates an ice-laden masterpiece. The light still shines, even through thick ice.

COOLEST SPORT
ICE SWIMMING

The water temperature is just above freezing, but for these hardy folks that's all part of the fun. Ice swimmers dive into frigid waters of 41°F (5°C) or less without a wet suit or other protections against the cold and then race against each other by swimming frigid laps. Some even take to the water for a mile (1.6 km) or more! Maybe these hardcore athletes should be called "cold-core" competitors.

COOLEST OVERNIGHT
ICEHOTEL, JUKKASJÄRVI, SWEDEN

Visitors to this hotel in northern Sweden sleep surrounded by ice, in rooms kept at 18 to 23°F (-8 to -5°C). Guests at the Icehotel, located about 120 miles (200 km) north of the Arctic Circle, can arrive on dogsled from the airport, take a ride on a reindeer sleigh, and sculpt their own block of ice. Reindeer hides and thermal sleeping bags keep the chill away, and a hot cup of lingonberry tea starts off the day.

COOLEST SOUNDS
ICE MUSIC FESTIVAL, GEILO, NORWAY

Musicians at this music festival in the mountains of southern Norway tune their instruments while wearing gloves. Why? The instruments are made out of ice just hours before the performance, and body heat can change their shapes and sounds. Festivalgoers listen to tunes in an igloo and rock out to ice drums, ice bass, and the iceofon (think "xylophone" made of ice). Reindeer skins keep the audience warm in the bone-chilling 5°F (-15°C) temperatures.

COOLEST 159

THE GREAT STALACPIPE **ORGAN** IS CONNECTED TO **37** **STALACTITES.**

GREAT STALACPIPE
ORGAN

This pipe organ isn't just large, it's cavernous ... literally! The Great Stalacpipe Organ, located in Luray Caverns, Virginia, U.S.A., is the world's largest natural musical instrument. Its supercool cave setting—and the story behind it—is what makes this melodious record breaker so unusual.

Before 1878, nobody knew the cave even existed. That year a few men felt chilly air blowing out of a sinkhole at the top of a large hill. After a few hours of exploring, they discovered an entrance to the underground cave system. And what a place they found: a subterranean wonderland full of strange formations—mineral deposits called stalactites and stalagmites—that seemed to be dripping from the cave roof and rising from its floors. And there was a lot to discover: The caverns spread across an area the size of 48 football fields!

Decades later, an accomplished organist named Leland Sprinkle was visiting the cave with his five-year-old son, Robert, when a tour guide happened to tap a few stalactites to play the tune "Mary Had a Little Lamb." This gave Leland the idea for the unusual organ, and—after three years of searching for the stalactites that would sound just the right pitches—his amazing invention debuted in 1957. The electrical instrument uses parts of a regular organ, but instead of regular organ pipes, it works when small rubber "hammers" tap out the tunes on the cave formations. These musical "pipes" stretch throughout three acres (1.2 ha) of the cavern, and the sounds they make when struck are relayed back to the main organ console through a series of wires. Talk about living in harmony with nature!

FANTASTIC FORMATIONS

Luray Caverns' formations are made of calcite, a form of limestone. As rainwater percolates through the cave, it becomes slightly acidic. Then, as the water comes into contact with the air in the cave, the calcite "falls" out and covers the cave surfaces. Over millions of years these formations (known as speleothems) grow bigger and bigger. Stalactites hold tight to the cave ceiling, whereas stalagmites grow from the bottom— they are formed by dripping water coming off a stalactite or the cave wall itself.

THINK
PINK

Is it half baby chick ... half worm? Or a hamster on a half shell? Neither! This cool and compact creature is the pink fairy armadillo—the smallest armadillo in the world. Five-inch (13-cm)-long *Chlamyphorus truncatus* lives in the grasslands and shrubby plains of central Argentina. If threatened, these mini mammals—which weigh only about 3.5 ounces (100 grams), about the same as two candy bars—use their large, specialized claws to bury themselves within seconds in the sandy soils of their home. Their claws, though handy for their frequent burrowing, make it hard for them to walk on hard ground; their tiny tails help the creatures balance by acting as a sort of "fifth limb." The armadillo's rosy color comes from blood pumped into its shell, which helps it to cool down. If the armadillo needs to stay warm, it pumps the blood back out.

THE END OF THE PINK FAIRY ARMADILLO'S ONE-INCH (2.5-CM)-LONG TAIL IS SHAPED LIKE A DIAMOND.

Scientists don't really understand the diet of the nocturnal armadillo well enough to feed it in captivity. (Sadly, most die within days of being captured.) One researcher fed a captive critter that couldn't be returned to the wild a mixture of cat food, milk, and a banana, which it slurped up for eight months. But the next time she tried to feed this mixture to another armadillo, it turned up its nose.

COOL VS. COOLER

Get ready to rumble! Only one of these zany matchups can be crowned number one in the category of cool.

FLYING CAMERAS VS. FLYING SOLO

WINNER

WHY FLYING CAMERAS ARE COOL: "AirSelfie" hovers in the air to let you take selfies and videos of all your friends from 65 feet (20 m) up—so no more pulled muscles from trying to get everyone in the picture.

WHY FLYING SOLO IS COOLER: What if you could take to the air by strapping on a jet pack to fly above the scene to record it? JetPack Aviation has been testing lightweight engines and airframes for more than 40 years in the hope of making that dream a reality.

ICE FLOWERS VS. CHERRY BLOSSOMS

WHY ICE FLOWERS ARE COOL: These beauties are made up of delicate threads of ice. Some plant stems sprout "ice" flowers when conditions are just right—when the air is below freezing but the soil temperature is slightly warmer.

WHY CHERRY BLOSSOMS ARE COOLER: Cherry blossoms require only a change of season to burst into pink flowers. People in Japan have been viewing the blooms for more than a thousand years in rituals to celebrate the new life that happens every spring.

WINNER

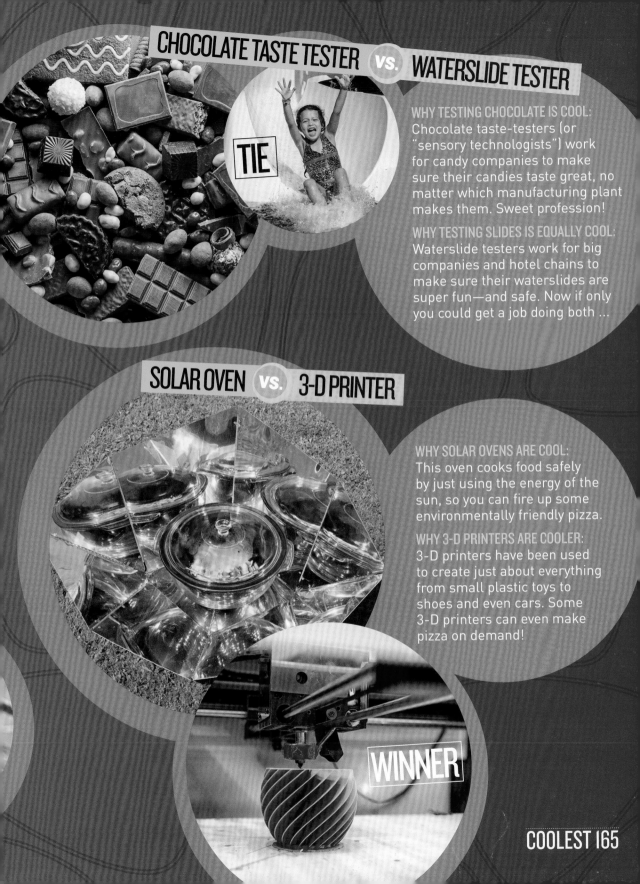

CHOCOLATE TASTE TESTER vs. WATERSLIDE TESTER

TIE

WHY TESTING CHOCOLATE IS COOL: Chocolate taste-testers (or "sensory technologists") work for candy companies to make sure their candies taste great, no matter which manufacturing plant makes them. Sweet profession!

WHY TESTING SLIDES IS EQUALLY COOL: Waterslide testers work for big companies and hotel chains to make sure their waterslides are super fun—and safe. Now if only you could get a job doing both ...

SOLAR OVEN vs. 3-D PRINTER

WHY SOLAR OVENS ARE COOL: This oven cooks food safely by just using the energy of the sun, so you can fire up some environmentally friendly pizza.

WHY 3-D PRINTERS ARE COOLER: 3-D printers have been used to create just about everything from small plastic toys to shoes and even cars. Some 3-D printers can even make pizza on demand!

WINNER

RECORD-BREAKING
SWEETS

Time taken
to eat two pounds
(0.9 kg) of
chocolate
candy bars
6 minutes

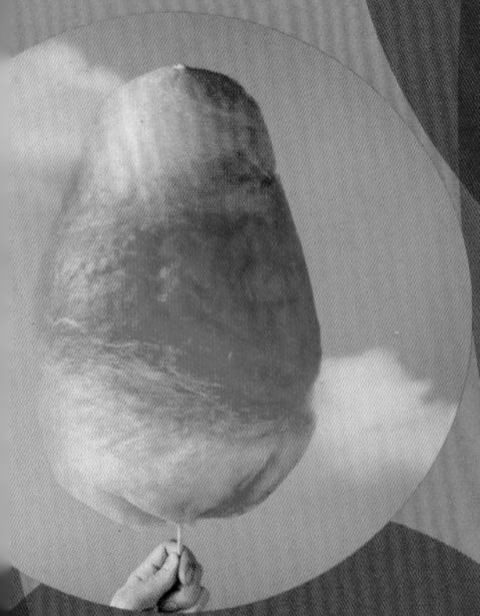

Tallest cotton candy
**17 feet
10.57 inches
(5.45 m)**

Largest taffy
**1,000 feet +
(305 m) long
524 pounds
(237.68 kg)**

166

Largest candy mosaic
300,000 pieces of candy

Heaviest chocolate bar
13 feet 1.48 inches (4 m) long, 12,770 pounds 4.48 ounces (5,792.5 kg)

Number of M&M's eaten in one minute using chopsticks
65

Number of ice-cream scoops balanced on one cone
121

SUPREMELY COOL GENIUS

Leonardo da Vinci, a groundbreaking artist and inventor in 15th-century Italy, could do just about everything. He had talents and capabilities in a wide range of subjects, from science and mathematics to more artistic pursuits like painting and sketching.

Born April 15, 1452, in Vinci, Italy (which is why he is now known as Leonardo da Vinci), he showed promise as an artist from an early age. That talent would create what might be the most famous piece of art in the world: the "Mona Lisa," painted sometime between 1503 and da Vinci's death, in 1519. But creating that masterpiece is only one of many things the famous left-hander accomplished. Leonardo built a silver lyre (a musical instrument), and he sketched out plans for an armored tank,

a submarine, a flying machine, and an early form of a bicycle. He also drew detailed studies of the human body, plants, and animals. As an engineer, he designed churches and canals.

But having such a far-ranging mind meant that Leonardo wasn't always tidy. He'd fill notebooks with scientific observations and illustrations for machines he invented in his head. One drawing discovered in 2016 had a sketch for a painting on one side and studies of candlelight on the other. Sometimes he would draw on loose pieces of paper and stick them in his belt. And Leonardo would also start paintings or sculptures and then not finish them, sometimes because of the events of the day or maybe his interests would just move on. But that's OK. Even geniuses aren't perfect!

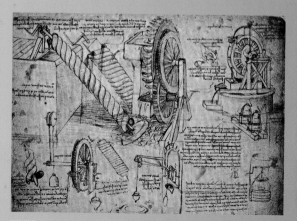

LEONARDO CREATED A MECHANICAL LION IN WHICH A BOUQUET OF LILIES CAME OUT WHEN ITS CHEST WAS OPENED.

NAME: Leonardo da Vinci
BORN: April 15, 1452, in Italy
DIED: May 2, 1519, in France
PROFESSION: Engineer,
architect, sculptor, painter
NUMBER OF KNOWN
DRAWINGS: Nearly 2,500

COOLEST 169

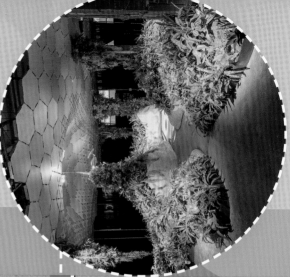

COOL AT A GLANCE

PUFFER FISH CREATIONS

The astonishing puffer fish "sand" sculptures are wondrous works of art. The male fish will spend up to nine days to craft the expressive circles, using his fins as paintbrushes to move around the sand into elaborate patterns.

1 COOLEST PLACE TO TAKE A SELFIE

After you take a selfie from the glass observation deck at the Willis Tower skyscraper in Chicago, Illinois, U.S.A., be sure to look down—all 103 stories! At this scenic spot, visitors stand 1,353 feet (412 m) above the ground with nothing but a see-through box between them and the city below. On a clear day, Skydeck Chicago offers views of Chicago and into four different states.

2 COOLEST ANIMAL ART

And the award goes to ... male puffer fish! The five-inch (12-cm)-long fish create elaborate circles in the sand that can stretch for seven feet (2 m). Why? These underwater "crop" circles are not just for show—they are used to attract a mate.

3 COOLEST UNDERGROUND PARK

This park will be the tops ... if you can be the "tops" underground! Developers of the Lowline—projected to open in 2021—envision turning a one-acre (0.4-ha) space underneath New York City streets into a subterranean world of walking paths and green plants that will grow from sunlight captured from the streets above. It's a new twist for a space that used to be where trolley cars would turn around on their routes.

4 | COOLEST COLLECTION

It's not the location of this Svalbard seed vault—on Norway's Svalbard archipelago—that makes it so cool, even though it is in the frigid Arctic. What's inside is even cooler: seeds from approximately 4.5 million different kinds of plants. Some 394 feet (120 m) deep inside a snow-covered mountain, the vault's location in the permafrost keeps them perma-safe.

5 | COOLEST INVENTION

This levitating lightbulb hovers above its base and emits energy-efficient LED light. Now that's a bright idea! The forces of electromagnetism keep the bulb aloft.

6 | COOLEST SWING

This swing isn't for the faint of heart. The supersize swing at Glenwood Caverns Adventure Park in Colorado, U.S.A., launches four riders 1,300 feet (396 m) over Glenwood Canyon, reaching speeds of 50 miles an hour (80 km/h). Far out!

COOL
AND CONNECTED

A h, the Internet—imagine a world without it. Impossible? This incredible invention links people all over the planet. It allows us to watch movies and listen to music from our laptop, look up information for school papers, and talk to grandparents from far away. Its invention revolutionized not only how we communicate but also how we spend our time. It may seem like it has been around forever, but that's not the case.

In the 1960s, scientists and engineers started to work on getting computers to "talk" to one another as a way to aid their research. Soon, computers in Los Angeles, Stanford, and Santa Barbara, California, were linked to a fourth one in Salt Lake City, Utah, through a U.S. government program called ARPANET. An early form of the Internet was born. And once it was unleashed, there was no turning back!

But it wasn't always smooth sailing. From the start, researchers used this network to communicate with one another. (Email was introduced in 1972—now that's old!) But different computer operating systems and lots of different software meant that communication could become a huge headache, as people struggled to work with different programs. Then, in 1989, a British scientist named Tim Berners-Lee, who was working at a physics laboratory called CERN in Geneva, Switzerland, created a program that gave computers a common set of standards—a common "language"—and anyone who wanted to use it could use it. This language includes "http" addresses, HTML coding, and URLs. This standard platform, known as the World Wide Web, took the headache out of the Internet.

ABOUT HALF THE WORLD'S POPULATION IS ONLINE.

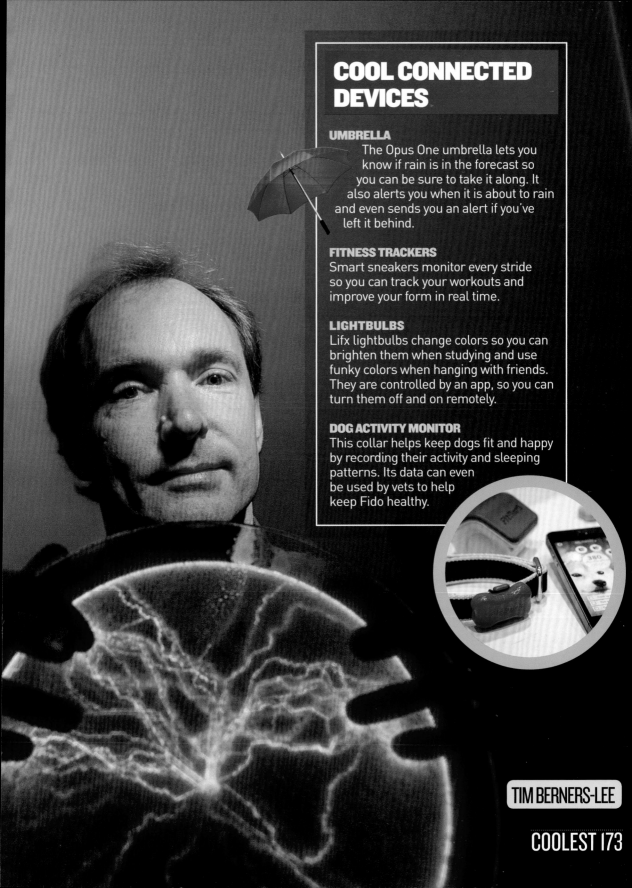

COOL CONNECTED DEVICES

UMBRELLA
The Opus One umbrella lets you know if rain is in the forecast so you can be sure to take it along. It also alerts you when it is about to rain and even sends you an alert if you've left it behind.

FITNESS TRACKERS
Smart sneakers monitor every stride so you can track your workouts and improve your form in real time.

LIGHTBULBS
Lifx lightbulbs change colors so you can brighten them when studying and use funky colors when hanging with friends. They are controlled by an app, so you can turn them off and on remotely.

DOG ACTIVITY MONITOR
This collar helps keep dogs fit and happy by recording their activity and sleeping patterns. Its data can even be used by vets to help keep Fido healthy.

TIM BERNERS-LEE

COOL CLOSE-UPS

Can you identify these mega famous landmarks up close?

1

2

3

4

COOLEST 175

CHAPTER 7

WE'VE **SAVED** THE **MOST EXTREME** RECORD BREAKERS **FOR LAST.**

There's no doubt about it—the features in this chapter are no average Joes! From scorching crystal caves to supertough tardigrades to an airport that's a real cliff-hanger, you're going to want to hold on to your hat for this show-and-tell of epic proportions!

THE MOST EXTREME CAVE ON EARTH

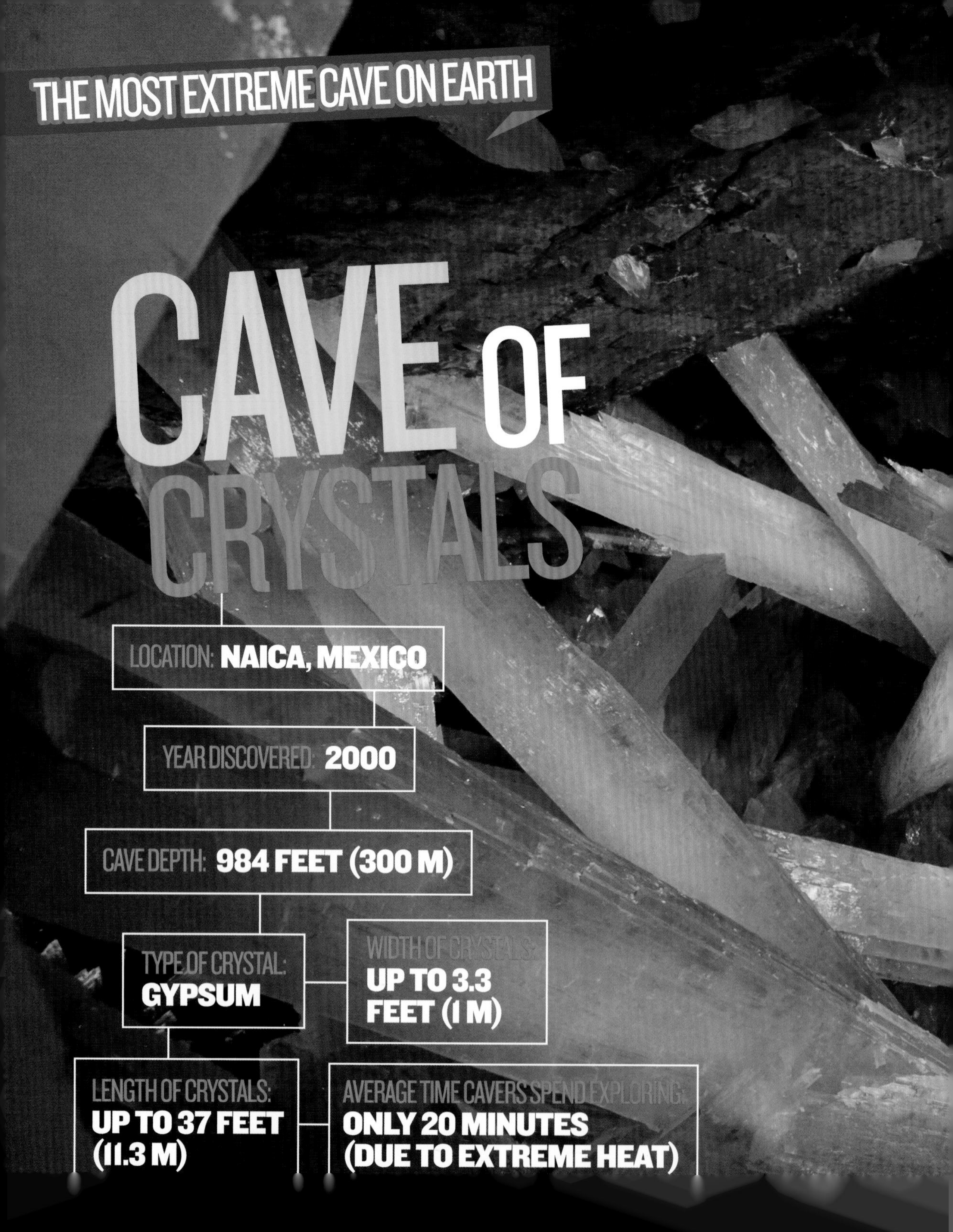

CAVE OF CRYSTALS

LOCATION: **NAICA, MEXICO**

YEAR DISCOVERED: **2000**

CAVE DEPTH: **984 FEET (300 M)**

TYPE OF CRYSTAL: **GYPSUM**

WIDTH OF CRYSTALS: **UP TO 3.3 FEET (1 M)**

LENGTH OF CRYSTALS: **UP TO 37 FEET (11.3 M)**

AVERAGE TIME CAVERS SPEND EXPLORING: **ONLY 20 MINUTES (DUE TO EXTREME HEAT)**

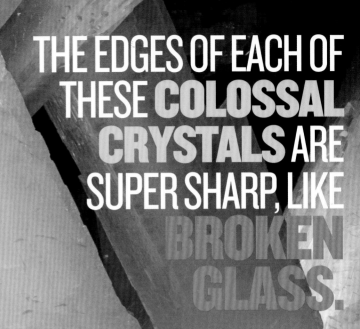

THE EDGES OF EACH OF THESE **COLOSSAL CRYSTALS** ARE SUPER SHARP, LIKE BROKEN GLASS.

The Cave of Crystals in Naica, Mexico, is an incredible sight to behold. But before cavers can enter this extreme environment, they have to suit up with special jumpsuits and strap on a backpack that pumps ice-cold air into their respirator masks to keep them cool: The cave temperature is 118°F (48°C) with 90 percent humidity! The Naica Caves were first opened by miners looking for silver and other metals more than 100 years ago, but it wasn't until 2000 that the deep "Crystal Cave" was discovered. The heat down there may be too hot to handle for most, but the payoff is huge—literally!—for the few researchers the mine owners allow to enter: The cave contains some of the world's largest crystals, as long as 37 feet (11.3 m) and weighing up to a staggering 44 tons (40 t). Better watch your step when exploring this *hot* cave!

EXTREME AGILITY

These winners really push the boundaries!

MOST EXTREME CLIMBING

ALEX HONNOLD

Rock climber Alex Honnold seems to defy gravity, often climbing the most technical routes without the use of ropes or any other safety equipment, which is called free-soloing. In 2017 he became the first person to free-solo the 3,000-foot (914-m) granite wall of El Capitan in Yosemite Valley, in California, U.S.A., using just a bag of chalk to help his hands grip the slippery rock.

ALEX HONNOLD CLIMBS ON THE EAST COAST OF THE MUSANDAM PENINSULA IN OMAN.

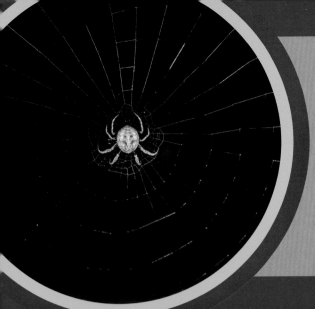

MOST EXTREME **SPINNING**

BARK SPIDERS

Found in Madagascar and South Africa, Darwin's bark spiders can spin webs reaching 82 feet (25 m) across—about as long as two city buses. Their webs have even been found stretching across a river! These mega webs are not only supersize, they're also superstrong: The silk is as tough as the material used to make bullet-proof vests.

MOST EXTREME **RUNNING**

GREAT WALL MARATHON

Covering a marathon's 26.2 miles (42.2 km) is tough enough, but add in 5,164 stairs and an "ordinary" marathon becomes extreme. Considered one of the most challenging races in the world, the course of the Great Wall Marathon covers part of the famous landmark in China, including the historic stone steps. Starting at the Huangyaguan section of the Great Wall in Tianjin city, runners trek through farmlands and villages, and even run a section of the wall itself.

MOST EXTREME **JUMPING**

MAKO SHARKS

Talk about a fish out of water! Mako sharks can jump an incredible 20 feet (6 m) above the ocean's surface. Twelve feet (3.7 m) long and weighing in at more than 1,200 pounds (544 kg), Mako sharks can swim up to 60 miles an hour (97 km/h), giving them plenty of speed to burst from the sea.

These four incredible sights take it to the limit.

MOST EXTREME
SOLAR POWER
SOLAR IMPULSE 2

During 2015 and 2016, two pilots took turns flying a powerful plane around the world. Why is that extreme? Because their cool craft runs on the sun! The Solar Impulse 2 left from Abu Dhabi, United Arab Emirates, and flew for 25,850 miles (40,000 km) in 17 different stages. A record-breaking five-day—and night—flight from Japan to Hawaii showed just how long this exceptional plane could fly, powered only by the clean energy of the sun.

MOST EXTREME ARCHITECTURE
THE PIANO BUILDING

A building in Huainan, China, tops the scales—the musical scales that is! The black and transparent glass structure looks just like a giant piano and violin. Visitors ride an escalator in the violin to reach the concert halls and rooms within the piano. The architectural wonder even has a rooftop patio and can light up at night.

MOST EXTREME **AIRPORT**

JUANCHO E. YRAUSQUIN AIRPORT

There's little room for error when pilots land at this airport on the island of Saba in the Caribbean Sea. The small landing strip is only a quarter of a mile (400 m) long, with steep cliffs falling to the sea on both ends of the runway. But that's not the only thing that makes this location so extreme: The steep hills surrounding the airport can cause sudden shifts in the winds, making for one tricky landing.

MOST EXTREME **POOL**

DEVIL'S POOL

Located at the top of Victoria Falls, on the border of Zambia and Zimbabwe, this extreme pool lets swimmers get up close to the 354-foot (108-m) waterfall without having to worry about toppling over the sheer drop, which is just a few feet away. Talk about edgy! Known as the Devil's Pool, a natural indention in the rock has a "lip" that protects swimmers from slipping over the brink. Victoria Falls also has its own extremes. The spray from the waterfall can be seen for 12 miles (20 km)!

DEATH VALLEY:
A DESERT OF EXTREMES

Death Valley, located in California and Nevada, U.S.A., is the hottest, driest, and lowest place in North America. Everything from its weather to its plants to its animals is extreme!

EXTREME HIGHS AND LOWS

The world record for highest air temperature—134°F (57°C)—was recorded at Death Valley's Furnace Creek in 1913. The area's coldest temperature—15°F (-10°C)—was also recorded at Furnace Creek ... the same year!

AS LOW AS YOU CAN GO

With an elevation of -282 feet (-86 m), Death Valley's Badwater Basin is the lowest point in North America. The basin comprises nearly 200 square miles (518 sq km) of salt flats. Minerals that dissolve from rocks during floods from distant mountain peaks make their way here. Once the minerals concentrate, the salts are all that remain. These conditions make it too harsh for most plants and animals to survive.

HEARTY PLANTS

Believe it or not, plants can survive in this hot, arid desert. In fact, one of the longest-living species of trees, the bristlecone pine, calls Death Valley home. Living up to 4,700 years, these trees don't need much water to survive; during dry periods, they go dormant until conditions improve. The tenacious tree even has an extreme exterior: gnarled, twisted branches and dark purple cones with prickles.

ADAPTABLE ANIMALS

Death Valley may not sound like the most comfortable place for *humans* to live year-round, but hundreds of species of animals have adapted to the extremes enough to call it home. Kangaroo rats never need to drink fresh water; they get all the liquids they need from their vegetarian diet, eating mostly seeds. And during the hottest time of year, the desert tortoise digs a burrow and enters a state of dormancy to conserve energy.

EXTREMOPHILES

Extremophiles are organisms that have chosen some seriously intense places to call home. With unique adaptations, they have found niches where few other organisms could survive.

TUBE WORMS

These aquatic annelids (worms) live at the edge of deep-sea thermal vents on the ocean's floor, where they can survive superheated water filled with toxic chemicals. Capable of living more than a mile (1.6 km) below the ocean's surface, the up-to-eight-feet (2.4-m)-long invertebrates have adapted to life under high pressure with zero sunlight.

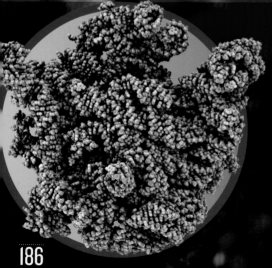

"CONAN THE BACTERIUM"

Deinococcus radiodurans, also known as "Conan the Bacterium," is a one-celled organism that can withstand extreme dryness, ultraviolet light, and acidic conditions. Accidentally discovered in 1956 by researchers who were studying spoiled canned meat, it has since been found to repair its own broken DNA. But what it is most famous for is being able to survive extreme levels of radiation—3,000 times as much as humans can. Scientists studying the extremophile are hoping to gain insight into protecting people from various types of radiation exposure, such as sun damage.

BRINE SHRIMP

Shrimpy doesn't mean wimpy! Brine shrimp in Utah, U.S.A.'s Great Salt Lake thrive in waters 10 times saltier than the ocean. How do they do it? Their outer body is waterproof, so salt water enters their body only through their mouth. The shrimp's gills and a special gland filter the salt out and help keep their system balanced.

SNOTTITES

Perhaps the best name of any extremophile, cave-dwelling snottites are slimy stalactites made of bacteria that look like, well, snot. The single-celled bacteria, which consume hydrogen sulfide gas and other noxious chemicals, hang on the walls and ceilings of caves, never seeing the light of day.

TARDIGRADES

Tardigrades, also known as water bears or moss piglets, are tiny, .04-inch (1-mm)-long invertebrates. Strangely adorable, they can live in intense environments, as they are able to survive in temperatures as low as -328°F (-200°C) and as high as 304°F (151°C). They can also withstand high doses of radiation and can go 10 years without water!

EXTREME SURVIVAL

ON MAY 29, 1953, SHERPA TENZING NORGAY AND NEW ZEALANDER EDMUND HILLARY BECAME THE FIRST PEOPLE TO REACH THE SUMMIT OF MOUNT EVEREST.

When it comes to going the distance, Sherpas are extreme experts. This group of Himalayan people live in Nepal and parts of Tibet among the tallest mountains in the world, including the tallest of them all: Mount Everest. Known for their supreme skills at assisting climbers, Sherpas are able to ascend to extreme elevations and carry heavy loads that would thoroughly fatigue other people.

So what makes Sherpas so special? Oxygen levels at Everest's summit are a third less than those at sea level, and that makes climbing harder and much more dangerous than just a strenuous hike. Because Sherpas have lived at high elevations for centuries, their bodies have become used to lower oxygen levels, which has shaped them into endurance machines. Researchers recently found that the difference can even be seen on a cellular level: The Sherpas' mitochondria, the powerhouses of our cells, are more efficient at using oxygen than those of people who don't live at such heights. And that's not all: Sherpas also have the ability to keep their blood circulating to muscles and organs at a fast pace, even when it slows down for other people. Now that's an amazing adaptation!

RECORD-BREAKING FAMILY

In May 24, 2003, 15-year-old Ming Kipa Sherpa became the youngest girl to stand on the summit of 29,035-foot (8,850-m)-tall Mount Everest. And she wasn't alone. Her 30-year-old sister, Lhakpa Sherpa, and her 24-year-old brother, Mingma Gelu Sherpa, climbed with her. Lhakpa also broke a record that year, becoming the first woman to summit three times. In 2017 Lhakpa broke her own record, again—this time reaching the summit for the eighth time. Mingma has summited eight times, too. This is one high-achieving family!

THESE NESTS ARE
SO **WELL BUILT**
THEY CAN LAST
FOR A CENTURY.

SOCIABLE WEAVERS' SUPERSIZE NESTS

These birds give new meaning to "extreme home makeover"! Africa's sociable weaverbirds work in large groups of about 500 to turn a tree into a community nest, which can ultimately weigh more than 2,000 pounds (907 kg) and measure 20 feet (6 m) long by 13 feet (4 m) wide and 7 feet (2 m) thick. A nest may contain 100 chambers, or individual apartments, for mating pairs. These nests—the largest built on Earth—are so heavy they have been known to collapse a tree!

You wouldn't guess these massive bird condos were nests at first glance—they look more like enormous haystacks teetering on the tops of trees. They are typically built in trees with long, smooth trunks and high branches to discourage cobras from slithering in. What a cleverly constructed coop!

EACH NEW GENERATION OF BIRDS IN A FAMILY BUILDS ON THE SAME NEST.

ULTIMATE FACE-OFF

Find out which extreme will excel in this smackdown to end all smackdowns.

KILAUEA VOLCANO **VS.** YELLOWSTONE SUPERVOLCANO

Stand back! Hawaii's Kilauea volcano is one of the most active volcanoes on Earth, erupting nearly continuously since 1983. Yellowstone volcano hasn't erupted for 174,000 years, but it is a *super-volcano*; if it did erupt, it would blow bigger than Kilauea ever could, capable of an eruption of more than 240 cubic miles (1,000 cubic km) of magma. This catastrophe would cause falling ash over several U.S. states and short-term changes to global climate.

WINNER

NORTH POLE **VS.** SOUTH POLE

Brrrr! Situated at opposite ends of Earth, you'd think the North and South Pole would tie for extreme. At both poles the sun never rises more than 23.5 degrees above the horizon, and they both have six months of continuous darkness. But Antarctica's South Pole experiences more extreme cold. Here's why: It sits on top of a thick ice sheet, which sits on the continent. The average winter temperature at the South Pole is -76°F (-60°C); at the North Pole, it's a balmy -40°F (-40°C).

WINNER

BURLY BREAKFAST BURRITO vs. MEGA PIZZA

WINNER

Better bring an appetite to this throw-down! Big Pie in the Sky Pizzeria in Georgia, U.S.A., serves up an "XL" pizza that is 30 inches (0.8 m) across—almost twice as wide as a typical large pizza. At Denver, Colorado's Jack-n-Grill, they serve a 7-pound (3.2-kg) burrito, made up of 7 potatoes, 12 eggs, a whole onion, cheese, and a pound (.45 kg) of ham. It may not be as big as the pizza, but the burrito wins the battle. Why? It's meant to be eaten by one—not shared like a pizza!

A RUBBER DUCK vs. A TALL HAND

A bird in the hand is worth two in the bush, the saying goes— meaning it's better to hold on to something you have rather than trading up for something better. But what if the bird is too *big* to fit in the hand? Standing 61 feet (18.6 m) high and 85 feet (25.9 m) wide, the largest rubber duck in the world has floated in harbors around the world. The world's largest hand sculpture, La Mano del Desierto, in Chile's Atacama Desert, is a mere 36 feet (11 m) tall—too short to get the thumbs up to win this competition.

WINNER

GOING TO EXTREMES
IN THE DEEP BLUE SEA

If you think the extremes on land are intense, you should check out what's going on below the surface of the ocean!

3,280 feet (1,000 m)
Deepest that sunlight can reach in the ocean

400 feet (122 m)
Deepest dive without scuba gear (free dive)

9,816 feet (2,992 m)
Deepest diving marine mammal (the Cuvier's beaked whale)

18,904 feet (5,762 m)
Deepest shipwreck (German cargo ship *Rio Grande*)

6.8 miles (10.9 km)
Deepest spot in the ocean: Challenger Deep, western Pacific Ocean

5 miles (8 km)
Deepest swimming fish (6-inch [15-cm] snailfish)

ERNEST SHACKLETON: EXTREME EXPLORER

Ernest Shackleton is the hero of an epic tale of extreme survival and perseverance. This Irish-English explorer commanded the Imperial Trans-Antarctic Expedition on a quest to be the first team to cross Antarctica. What happened on their journey might seem like a whale of a tale, but it's all true.

In October 1914, Shackleton and his crew sailed from Buenos Aires, Argentina, to the frozen continent. It showed them little mercy: Their ship, the *Endurance,* became trapped in the ice by January 1915, and for 10 months the team waited it out, drifting on the ice. When the thaw began, it splintered the wooden ship, which slowly sank in November. The 28 men then lived for six months drifting on an ice floe before eventually making it to mountainous and remote Elephant Island by sailing in three lifeboats for seven days. There they lived among the penguins and seals, stuck off the Antarctic coast.

In April 1916, because winter was coming (the seasons are reversed in the Southern Hemisphere), Shackleton knew that to have any chance of survival they'd need to seek help at the closest settlement—a remote whaling station located on South Georgia Island. Shackleton and five men sailed in a lifeboat for the 800-mile (1,300-km) journey, battling 52-feet (16-m) waves in what are considered the most dangerous seas in the world. It took them 16 days.

When they finally reached South Georgia Island, the crew landed on the uninhabited side opposite the whaling station. That didn't stop Shackleton. To reach the help they sought, they would have to set out again—this time on foot—for miles across mountains and glaciers. Exhausted, frostbitten, and hungry, he and two others hiked their way across inhospitable, uncharted, perilous terrain. After 36 hours, they finally reached the station; a rescue effort was launched and all 27 men in his crew were eventually saved. Shackleton had not achieved his goal of crossing Antarctica, but this inspirational tale of human survival under the most extreme conditions has become one of the greatest adventure stories of all time.

POLAR PERSEVERANCE

The race to the South Pole was also one of supreme endurance. In the early 20th century, two teams vied to reach the bottom of the world—one led by the Norwegian Roald Amundsen, and one by British explorer Robert Falcon Scott. Amundsen reached the South Pole first, on December 14, 1911, a month before Scott's party. Sadly, Scott's party, totally exhausted and suffering from frostbite and lack of supplies, perished on the return trip.

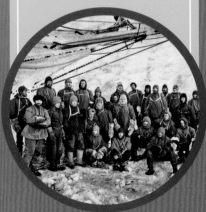

ERNEST SHACKLETON **JOINED** THE **MERCHANT NAVY** WHEN HE WAS JUST **16 YEARS OLD.**

ERNEST SHACKLETON

BORN: February 15, 1874

DIED: January 5, 1922

NUMBER OF PEOPLE WHO APPLIED TO GO ON THE ENDURANCE EXPEDITION: 5,000

NAME OF ENDURANCE LIFEBOATS: James Caird, Dudley Docker, Stancomb Wills

NAME OF THE TEAM'S CAMP ON ELEPHANT ISLAND: Patience

EXTREME AT A GLANCE

1 — MOST EXTREME ICE CREAM

There's frozen, and then there's *extremely* frozen. To turn cream into ice cream, some sweet shops use liquid nitrogen, a clear, colorless liquid that reaches temperatures of -320.8°F (-196°C). Because it freezes the cream instantaneously, ice cream is often transformed from liquid to frozen solid right in front of the customer!

2 — MOST EXTREME ZIP LINE

At 5,906 feet (1,800 m) long with a 2,000-foot (607-m) vertical drop and a maximum speed of 75 miles an hour (120 km/h), the ZipFlyer, near Pokhara, Nepal, is the longest, tallest, and steepest zip line in the world. Adventurers get a panorama view of the Himalaya on their epic ride.

3 — MOST EXTREME FRAGRANCE

Perfume scents are sometimes described as sweet or flowery. But how do you describe a perfume made from intestinal waste from a whale? Some say ambergris, collected from sperm whales, smells earthy or musky—even sweet. And it fetches a pretty penny: One pound (.45 kg) can be worth up to $63,000!

RACING TO SAVE A TOWN

In the winter of 1925, diphtheria broke out in the remote, icebound outpost of Nome, Alaska. Weather conditions prevented a train from bringing the serum needed to treat the sick the 674 miles (1,085 km) from the nearest town with medical supplies. But 20 teams of sled dogs were able to make the trek, saving the town. The trail they used to get there—the Iditarod Trail—is the same one Iditarod racers use today.

④ MOST EXTREME "BOAT" RACE

Most regattas involve row or sail boats, raced with precision. "Pumpkin regattas" take the sport to the extreme. Racers sit in a hollowed out giant pumpkin—some more than 1,000 pounds (454 kg)!—and steer using a kayak paddle. The first one to cross the finish line wins, but the greatest challenge isn't going fast—it's staying upright!

⑤ MOST EXTREME MIGRATION

Flying at extreme altitude, bar-headed geese migrate over the Himalaya, soaring as high as 24,000 feet (7,315 m)—about two-thirds as high as commercial jets fly. They can fly from sea level to 19,685 feet (6,000 m) in about eight hours at speeds of 40 miles an hour (64.5 km/h). And they are capable of constantly flapping their wings for up to 17 hours. Talk about frequent flyer miles!

⑥ MOST EXTREME SLED RACE

In well-below-freezing temperatures, racers in the Iditarod cover 1,000 miles (1,609 km) in as little as eight days with a team of sled dogs. The teams race day and night, traveling at speeds averaging 11 miles an hour (17.7 km/h) to reach their final destination—Nome, Alaska, U.S.A.

TURNING UP THE HEAT
IN THE NAME OF SCIENCE

The next time you take a bite of flaming-hot salsa, you might also be helping to fight cancer. The heat of some peppers is the stuff of eating competitions and chili cook-offs, but lurking behind the heat is a superpower: capsaicin. It's the component in chili peppers that makes your mouth feel like it's on fire. That intense feeling is measured in something called Scoville units, which is the scale researchers use to rank pepper potency. A green pepper is a 0 on the scale, and pure capsaicin is 16 million. Yowza!

How can you tell which peppers have the heat? The thinner the stem the hotter, and smaller-size peppers in a batch tend to be superb scorchers.

Scientists have found that the capsaicin in peppers has numerous potential medical benefits. The compound can be added to creams to help treat arthritis and some skin diseases that cause itching. Researchers have found that it could fight bacterial infections and possibly even some cancers. Capsaicin is also a great pain reliever—which might come in handy the next time you eat a piping hot pepper!

CHILI PEPPERS HAVE
MORE VITAMIN C
THAN ORANGES.

HOT TAKES

• The Carolina Reaper scores more than 1.569 million Scoville units.

• The seeds of hot peppers don't have capsaicin in them.

• Cinnamon and cilantro also contain capsaicin.

• Researchers who deal with capsaicin in its pure form have to wear gloves and a respirator.

• There are no poisonous hot peppers.

EXTREME 201

EXTREMELY EASY HOMEMADE VANILLA ICE CREAM

Want to whip up a batch of ice cream in a hurry? You can make this *extremely* delicious ice cream in a matter of minutes. Here's how!

INGREDIENTS

- 1 cup half-and-half
- 1/4 cup granulated sugar
- 1/2 teaspoon vanilla extract
- 2 cups crushed ice
- 3/4 cup rock salt

MATERIALS

- 1 quart-size resealable zipper plastic bag
- 1 gallon-size resealable zipper plastic bag

INSTRUCTIONS

1. Pour half-and-half, sugar, and vanilla into the quart-size bag, seal it well, and shake the bag vigorously until the ingredients are well-mixed.

2. Pour the ice and rock salt in the gallon-size bag, seal it well, and shake to mix it up.

3. Put the smaller bag (still zipped shut) in the large bag. Zip the large bag shut. Now it's time to dance around and shake that bag for a good five minutes. You can even toss it back and forth with a friend!

4. Let it rest for a few minutes, moving the ice around so the large bag is surrounding the small bag. This helps harden the ice cream. Open up the small bag with the ice cream, grab a spoon and dig in! Yum!

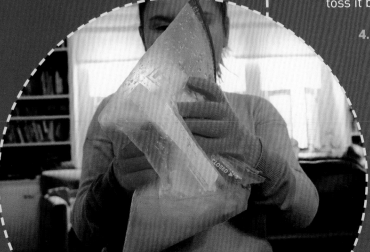

INDEX

Boldface indicates illustrations.

ILLUSTRATIONS
CREDITS

ASP = Alamy Stock Photo; DR = Dreamstime;
GI = Getty Images; IS: iStockphoto;
NGC = National Geographic Creative;
SS = Shutterstock

Cover: (Burj Khalifa), dblight/GI; (fennec fox),
Floridapfe/GI; (volcano), Carsten Peter/NGC;
(Jetpack), betoon/GI; Back cover: (giant rubber
duck), VCG/GI; (blue volcano), Godin Stphane/
hemis.fr RM/GI; (shark), Chris & Monique
Fallows/Nature Picture Library; Spine:
zhengalshuru/SS

Front matter: 1, FabioFilzi/Vetta/GI; 2-3,
Charlie Joe/Moment RF/GI; 4 (UP), SSSCCC/
SS; 4 (LO), Bertl123/SS; 5, Kuttelvaserova
Stuchelova/SS; 6-7, Carsten Peter /NGC

Chapter 1: 8-9, John Lund/Blend Images RM/
GI; 10-11, Rosenberg Philip/Perspectives/GI;
12, Kanuman/SS; 13, Danita Delimont/ASP; 13,
David Giral/ASP; 13 (CTR), asmithers/IS/GI;
14-15, Imaginechina/Newscom; 14 (LO), Solent
News/Splash News/Newscom; 14 (UP),
EcoPrint/SS; 15, pawel.gaul/IS/GI; 16,
Momentaryawe.com/Flickr RF/GI; 17 (UP LE),
Chan Srithaweeporn/Moment RM/GI; 17 (UP
RT), Gavin Hellier/AWL Images RM/GI; 17 (LO),
Yongyuan Dai/E+/GI; 18-19, PitK/SS; 18, Toru
Yamanaka/AFP/GI; 19 (UP), Chris Batson/ASP;
19 (LO), Six Flags Magic Mountain; 20-21, SPL/
Science Source; 20, Jaime Chirinos/Science
Source; 21 (LO), Suppakij1017/SS; 21 (CTR),
NASA/JPL/Science Source; 21 (UP), NASA,
ESA, and Erich Karkoschka (University of
Arizona)/Science Source; 22-23, Rebecca R
Jackrel/Flickr RF/GI; 24 (LO RT), Regien
Paassen/DR; 24 (UP LE), Amy Harris/DR; 24
(UP RT), S.Borisov/SS; 24 (LO LE), abzerit/IS/GI;
25 (UP LE), Entertainment Pictures/ASP; 25
(UP RT), Photo 12/ASP; 25 (LO LE), danm12/SS;
25 (LO RT), Soru Epotok/SS; 26-27, Mitsuaki
Iwago/Minden Pictures; 29, Trassnick/IS/GI; 30
(UP LE), Keith Bowser/ASP; 30-31 (LO), Paul
Harris/AWL Images RM/GI; 30 (LO), Feng Wei
Photography/Flickr RF/GI; 30 (UP RT),
FabioFilzi/E+/GI; 31 (LO RT), Thang Tat Nguyen/
Moment RF/GI; 31 (UP LE), zrfphoto/IS/GI; 31
(UP RT), Michael Durham/Minden Pictures;
32-33, Xinhua/Liu Xu/GI; 34 (LO), Stan Honda/
AFP/GI; 34 (UP LE), pawel.gaul/IS/GI; 35 (UP
LE), Paul Banton/DR; 35 (CTR), Samot/SS; 35
(UP RT), Naufal MQ/Moment RF/GI; 35 (LO LE),
LPETTET/IS/GI; 35 (LO RT), FabioFilzi/E+/GI

Chapter 2: 36-37, Shannon Hibberd/NGC;
38-39, Mark Thiessen/NGC; 40, Mariia
Goloviankо/SS; 41 (CTR), Makistock/SS; 41
(LO), Jennifer Cruce/EyeEm/GI; 41 (UP), Chip
Clark/Smithsonian Institution; 42-43,
ktsdesign/SS; 42, Scott Spitzer/University of
Pennsylvania; 43 (RT), MedicalRF.com/ASP; 43
(LE), Cornell University; 44 (UP), Astrid
Hinderks/ASP; 44, WENN.com/Newscom; 45
(LO), Tumbleweed Tiny House Company; 45
(CTR), Geoffrey de Ruiter; 45 (UP), SWNS; 46
(LO), Richard Leeney/Dorling Kindersley/GI; 46
(UP), AnatolyM/IS/GI; 47 (UP), Art_girl/SS; 47
(CTR), AnatolyM/IS/GI; 47 (LO), Dr. Robert
Lavinsky; 48-49, zrfphoto/IS/GI; 48 (LO),